Development of German Warplanes in WWI

A Centennial Perspective on Great War Airplanes and Seaplanes

Jack Herris

Great War Aviation Centennial Series #1

This book is dedicated to the pioneer aviators of WWI who fought in the first war in the air.

Acknowledgements

I want to especially thank Colin Owers for providing many of the contemporary aircraft photos from WWI and the Albatros D.Va in the Australian War Museum, the USAF Museum for photos of the aircraft in their collection, and Kenny Lisle for the photos of the Fokker Triplane replica in flight.

Cover photograph © Philip Makanna/GHOSTS. Please see his website: **www.ghosts.com**

Color aircraft profiles © Bob Pearson. Purchase his CD of WWI aircraft profiles for $50 US/Canadian, 40 €, or £30, airmail postage included, via Paypal to Bob at: **bpearson@kaien.net**

For our aviation books in print and electronic format, please see our website at: **www.aeronautbooks.com**. You may contact me at **jherris@verizon.net**.

An edition of this book designed for the iPad is available in the iTunes store; search ISBN **978-1-935881-50-6**

Interested in WWI aviation? Join The League of WWI Aviation Historians (**www.overthefront.com**) and Cross & Cockade International (**www.crossandcockade.com**).

Aeronaut Books

www.aeronautbooks.com

Table of Contents

Introduction	3
The *Frontbestand* Tables	7
Early Unarmed Aircraft	9
Miscellaneous	9
A Types	9
B Types	12
Armed Two-Seat Aircraft	16
C Types	16
Lichtbild Types	32
CL Types	32
J Types	37
S Types	43
N Types	44
Fighters	45
Monoplane Fighters (E Types)	45
Biplane Fighters (D Types)	50
Triplane Fighters (Dr Types)	66
The *Amerika* Program	72
The German Fighter Competitions	72
The Fokker D.VII	75
Second Fighter Competition	82
Third Fighter Competition	86
Bombers	88
G Types	88
R Types	100
GL Types	101
L Types	101
Force Composition	104
German Naval Aircraft	106
Naval Landplane Numbers	120
German Seaplane Numbers	124
Amerika Program Production Schedule	130
German Aircraft Manufacturers	133
German and Austrian Aircraft Engines	134
German Water-Cooled Inline Engines	134
German Air-Cooled Rotary Engines	136
Austrian Water-Cooled Inline Engines	138
German Aircraft Engine Manufacturers	140
Austrian Aircraft Engine Manufacturers	141
German Aircraft Inventory, 21 December 1917	142
German Warplane Production by Class	144
Bibliography	144
Glossary	145
Color Photos	148

Introduction

The purpose of this work is to describe and illustrate the development of German aircraft of WWI and to provide some context for understanding the design and procurement of these aircraft.

Within the German Army, *Idflieg* (*Inspektion der Fliegertruppen* – Inspectorate of military aviation) issued technical requirements and decided which aircraft were produced and in what quantity, and assigned aero engines to airframe manufacturers. Within the German Empire the state of Bavaria retained limited autonomy and sponsored the Pfalz Flugzeug Werke and the Rapp, later BMW, aero-engine producers that were located in Bavaria. Regardless, *Idflieg* had the final say in assignment of aero engines to airframe manufacturers, and *Idflieg* determined the policies and production of the German aviation industry.

The Antagonists

At the start of the war, the major combatants were the Central Powers (Germany and the Austro-Hungarian Empire) on one side, and the Allies (the British Empire, France, and Imperial Russia) on the other. As the war progressed, Bulgaria and the Ottoman Empire joined the Central Powers, and Italy and, much later, the United States joined the Allies.

Table 1 shows the population and annual steel production, a measure of industrialization, for the key powers at the start of hostilities. From these figures it is clear that Germany and the other Central Powers were at a great disadvantage in manpower in a war of attrition, and the Great War certainly developed into a war of attrition.

Table 1: Pre-War Industrial Potential

Country	Population including Colonies, Millions	Annual Steel Production (Million Tons)
Austria-Hungary	51.4	2.6
Germany	66.3	17.0
Total Central Powers	**117.7**	**19.6**
France	90.1	4.3
United Kingdom	422.7	10.0
Russian Empire	178	4.0
Total Allies	**690.8**	**18.3**

Note 1: Bulgaria and Turkey later joined the Central Powers; neither had significant industry and neither built aircraft during the war; all their aircraft were imported from Germany.

Note 2: Italy, Belgium, and later the United States must be added to the Allies. Belgium was over-run in the first days of the war, but Italy had a large population and a moderate industrial base. When America joined the Allies, it alone had 103 million people and produced three times as much steel as Germany and Austria-Hungary combined.

Germany and the Austro-Hungarian Empire were primarily land powers; both had huge and powerful armies. Germany also had a large navy, while her ally had a small navy. Russia and France also had large armies, and France also had a substantial navy. In contrast, Great Britain was the world's leading sea power yet had only a small army. The Royal Navy's imposition of a distant blockade the German High Seas Fleet was unable to break cut Germany off from access to imported raw materials while assuring the Allies had access to the world's raw materials. In the long term, the Royal Navy's distant blockade starved Germany of resources and ensured her defeat. Given the great imbalance in access to important raw materials and manpower, German defeat seems inevitable; the remarkable aspect is how Germany could manage to avoid defeat for so long.

The great imbalance in access to raw materials and manpower meant that, soon after the initial German advance in France and Belgium stalled into static trench warfare, the Germans realized they lacked the resources available to the Allies and always would. A German victory would necessarily depend on defeating the Allied armies in the field, especially on the Western Front, rather than winning a war of attrition. Unfortunately for Germany, there was no way to avoid a war of attrition, a war Germany could not win.

The impact of German manpower and material inferiority on German aviation was especially important to our story. In particular, permanent numerical inferiority forced the *Luftstreitkräfte* (German Air Service) on the strategic defensive early in the war and kept it there until the armistice. Numerical inferiority placed a priority on technical superiority, but achieving and maintaining technical superiority was difficult as both sides developed their aviation technology, tactics, and production as quickly as possible. In fact, technical superiority moved back and forth between Germany and the Allies, but the Allies consistently retained the numerical advantage.

Table 2 shows the aviation strength for key combatants at the beginning of the war. However, this was of transient importance as these primitive aircraft were quickly destroyed or worn out. More important was the ability of industry to replace these losses.

Table 2: Aviation Strength at Start of War

Country	Airplanes	Airships
Austria-Hungary	79	3
Germany	232	12
Total Central Powers	311	15
France	162	6
Russia	244	14
United Kingdom	113	6
Total Allies	519	26

Interestingly, Russia started the war with the largest number of aircraft. However, most of these were soon destroyed in the rigors of combat and Russian industry was unable to replace them in sufficient quantity or quality.

Table 3 gives total wartime aircraft and aero-engine production by country. This was far more significant to the war and clearly shows why German aviation went on the strategic defensive; Germany was always going to be outnumbered.

Table 3: WWI Aviation Production

Country	Airplanes	Aero Engines
Austria-Hungary	5,286	4,902
Germany	50,296	43,486
Total Central Powers	55,582	48,388
France	51,700	92,386
Italy	11,986	14,849
Russia	5,607	1,511
United Kingdom	52,027	41,034
United States	10,980	32,420
Total Allies	132,300	182,200
Total all countries	187,882	230,588

Aero engines, with their myriad of precision parts that must fit and work well together, are much harder to design and produce than airframes. Consequently, production of aero engines was the limiting factor in aircraft production. For example Russia, despite her huge army, was a minor aviation power because her lack of industrialization limited her aero engine production to far below requirements. Most aero engines used in Russia had to be imported from France. France exceeded all other powers in aero engine production and was critical to her allies for aero engines, completed aircraft, and aircraft and aero-engine designs that could be built under license.

Germany's situation lay between these extremes. Her production of aero engines was much less than desired and was easily exceeded by her airframe production, requiring re-cycling of aero engines to boost production. Worse yet, among Germany's allies only the Austro-Hungarian Empire built warplanes and aero engines, and those in inadequate numbers. This meant German aviation production, already insufficient for her own needs, had also to support her other allies, further stressing the German aviation effort.

As the war progressed, aircraft and aircrews became more capable and the importance of aviation continually increased. This put increasing demands on the aviation industries of all combatants, and German aviation production increasingly fell behind the French, British, and eventually the Americans, all of whom had access to far greater material and manpower resources.

Procurement Philosophy

The increasing demands on aviation and the different situations regarding available resources resulted in different procurement philosophies. The resource-rich Allies focused on developing a limited number of competent airframes and aero engines and maximizing production of those types. Contemporary photographs generally show Allied squadrons composed of a single aircraft type except when evaluating or transitioning to a new type.

In contrast, *Idflieg*, faced with permanent numerical inferiority, tried to maximize aircraft performance by producing airframes optimized for their roles. Contemporary photographs of German units, especially two-seater units, normally show a variety of different aircraft types, with different types assigned to different operational roles. This helps account for the great variety of different German aircraft types, about 650 different designs, compared to about 400 different aircraft designs produced by France and about 300 by Great Britain, despite the greater quantity of aircraft the Allies produced.

The comparatively large number of different designs by all combatants was also a result of the need to constantly try new concepts in flight; no computer simulations were available to explore design variations. Fokker alone produced 75 different aircraft types during the war in a constant search for better performance and combat effectiveness.

Idflieg attempted to limit the impact of numerical inferiority in the air by producing reliable, standard engines for maximum availability. For example, the six-cylinder Mercedes D.III engine that powered most German fighter designs was one of the most reliable of the time, enabling most assigned aircraft to fly on any given day. In contrast, the excellent Hispano-Suiza V-8 engine, which powered the best

Allied fighters, was frequently available for flight an average of only one day out of three due to serious maintenance issues. Despite the Hispano-Suiza's reliability problems, the Allies' numerical superiority, coupled with the engine's excellent performance when it was running properly, made the situation tolerable for the Allies; this problematic availability would not have been tolerable for Germany.

Another distinction between German and Allied designs was the type of engine used. The Allies used rotary engines widely throughout the war, although these were gradually replaced by powerful water-cooled engines as the war progressed and these more powerful engines became available. In contrast, German designs primarily used water-cooled engines of six-cylinder configuration throughout the war.

The rotary engine's sole advantage was its low weight for its power, a factor that was especially important early in the war when available engines produced only modest power. However, the rotary engine used a great deal of fuel and oil for its power, was relatively unreliable, and was constantly trying to tear itself apart when running. In fact, due to its inherent limitations, development of rotary engines essentially stopped after the war and the type soon disappeared. No wonder *Idflieg* preferred the more reliable straight-six engine that consumed much less precious fuel and oil for its power.

Initially German authorities considered the six-cylinder engine satisfactory for all classes of airplanes. However, its length was viewed as a disadvantage for fighters, and in early 1916 *Idflieg* and its engineering branch the *Flugzeugmeisterei* (Aviation Engineering Division) asked the engine industry to develop the shorter, more compact V-8 engine for fighter aircraft. The subsequent appearance of the Spad fighter with the Hispano-Suiza V-8 engine, followed by other Allied fighters with V-8 engines, was a major incentive for German industry to develop a V-8 for fighters. Both Benz and Daimler soon had running V-8 prototypes, initially without reduction gearing due to development problems. Later the gear problems were solved. However, development of the V-8 engine was too prolonged. Although production of V-8 engines started before the armistice and about 400 production engines were made by Benz and Daimler, but they were too late to reach the front.

Engines were successfully tested with superchargers, but these did not reach production during the war. Meanwhile, 'over-compressed' engines were used for high-altitude flight. These over-compressed engines could not be run at full throttle below 2,000 meters (6,562 feet) altitude without detonation and severe engine damage. Above 2,000 meters the engines could be run at full throttle, giving superior high-altitude performance compared to standard engines.

Although the rotary engine was comparatively rare in Germany, the innovative counter-rotary engine designed by Siemens-Halske deserves special mention. Standard rotary engines had their propeller attached to the engine block which rotated about a stationary crankshaft, with a typical speed of 1400 RPM. In the Siemens-Halske design the cylinders rotated in one direction at 900 RPM while the propeller rotated in the other direction at 900 RPM. This gave a relative speed of 1800 RPM for more power, plus a lower propeller speed of 900 RPM that was more efficient, allowing a massive propeller to be installed. The 160 hp Sh.III engine gave exceptional climb to the fighters that used it, and it was developed into the Sh.IIIa with 220–240 hp. Extensive development work on adequate engine cooling was required due to the slow cylinder rotation speed, which reduced airflow over the cylinders. Production fighters were initially plagued with engine failures due to overheating, and production of this exceptional engine was limited by development problems. Interestingly, Sh.III engines built under license by Rhemag were not affected by these problems.

An obvious question is, if the rotary had so many limitations, why not use radial engines instead? In fact, the radial engine was developed into the most powerful aircraft piston engine type during WW2.

Above: Early flight was hazardous at best, and stability was a prized attribute of primitive airplanes. The *Taube* (dove) wing planform offered great natural stability and many German designers used it for that reason. A small number of *Tauben* equipped German units at the beginning of the war, but the *Taube* was soon replaced by biplanes of greater performance. Despite its inherent stability, this one ended up on its nose while landing on a rough field.

The problem was the limitations of the alloys and mechanical designs available during WWI. The rotary had to spin its cylinders for cooling. The radial engines available in WWI had to be water-cooled; air cooling was not sufficient for the alloys and cylinder head designs of the time.

World War I aircraft were also characterized by the scarcity of multi-engine aircraft compared to later periods, and especially WW2 when multi-engine aircraft were common. Partly this was a result of the scarcity of engines and the need to conserve resources. The other reason was technical; the lack of ability to 'feather' the propeller of a failed engine. Starting in the 1920s, and standard by the late 1930s, multi-engine aircraft were equipped with propellers that could feather; that is, turn their blades perpendicular to the airflow if the engine failed, locking them in position and preventing them from rotating in the wind as the plane flies. This is essential, because a wind-milling propeller generates drag comparable to a parachute of the same diameter. Propellers of WWI aircraft were generally carved out of wood and could not be adjusted in flight. In event of an in-flight engine failure, the propeller wind-milled, creating extensive drag. In fact, the drag was so great that a twin-engine aircraft could not maintain level flight; all the running engine could do was extend the aircraft's glide.

This brief discussion points to the requirement for German *Reisenflugzeuge*, R-planes or giant airplanes, to be designed to allow in-flight engine maintenance. The drag associated with a wind-milling propeller is also the reason many R-planes were designed with central engine installations that enabled a failed engine to be de-coupled from driving the propellers via a clutch, allowing the running engines to turn all the propellers.

Summary

Throughout the war the German economy was increasingly strangled by the distant blockade of the Royal Navy, putting her aviation industry at a great disadvantage in raw materials. German aircraft and aero engine production was never enough to prevent Allied numerical superiority, forcing the German Air Service on the strategic defensive.

Constant numerical inferiority had pernicious affects on procurement policy. For example, once the Albatros fighters had achieved temporary technical superiority, German authorities became complacent, thinking their superiority was long-lasting, and ordered them in large quantities. When superior Allied fighters reached the front, Germany was in a quandary; making significant changes in design, especially aero engine design, now became essential, but changes could interrupt desperately needed production, further aggravating her numerical inferiority.

In another example, a constant shortage of aero engines forced Germany to power the heavy armored J-types with the 200 hp Benz instead of the more powerful 260 hp Mercedes D.IVa. This prevented them from using shorter fields and compromised their performance, maneuverability, and flight safety. In contrast, when the unarmored Liberty Plane arrived at the front it was powered by the 400 hp Liberty V-12 engine. Bringing the powerful Liberty engine into mass production in a matter of months was a great achievement not matched by the German aero engine industry.

Idflieg went on two destructive tangents by imitating successful Allied configurations. First was encouraging German manufacturers to utilize the Nieuport sesquiplane configuration. While this configuration had some advantages, the fact that it used a single-spar lower wing was a great structural weakness inherited by the German designs that used it. Some manufacturers went to the extreme of actually copying the Nieuport design, ensuring their aircraft would be outmoded before they reached the front.

The German triplane craze of 1917, when *Idflieg* encouraged German fighter manufacturers to explore the triplane configuration based on the success of the Sopwith Triplane, was also a dead end that wasted valuable time and design resources. Interestingly, the Sopwith Triplane was replaced in production and on operations by the Sopwith Camel biplane, which offered no performance improvement but carried two guns and was much stronger structurally than the delicate Triplane.

Confronted by an enemy with nearly unlimited resources, who could build far more aero engines, including advanced V-8 engines, Germany focused on innovative structural and aerodynamic design to compensate for the lower power of her six-cylinder aero engines. Although the Fokker D.VII achieved that, and the Junkers and Dornier all-metal aircraft were far in advance of Allied airframes, the comparative neglect of engine development was probably the biggest policy mistake *Idflieg* made; the engine is the heart of the airplane and determines its overall performance. A combination of structural and aerodynamic design and an excellent engine are needed for decisive technical superiority. Unfortunately, *Idflieg* relied too long on the reliable six-cylinder engines by Benz and Mercedes. Newer V-8 and V-12 engines were needed for technical superiority, but initial complacency delayed their development too long.

The Frontbestand Tables

In the discussions that follow, the *Frontbestand* tables will be given for each category of warplane. *Bestand* means inventory, supply, or strength, and *Frontbestand* signifies inventory at the front. In the case of these tables, that appears to include aircraft in frontline combat units, air parks, and repair units serving at the front and flying schools just behind the front, but not large flying schools in Germany.

The original information for the *Frontbestand* tables was taken from German Army Archives in 1920 for use by *Dr.-Ing.* Wilhelm Hoff, who used it to write an article "Die Entwicklung Deutscher Heeresflugzeug im Kriege" (The Development of German Army Aircraft in the War) published in the *Zeitschrift des Vereines Deutscher Ingenieure*, 1920, p.493. This is the only contemporary article on the subject. The data was in the Weyl collection (Weyl was Hoff's assistant in the 1920s) that Peter M. Grosz purchased in 1959. The *Frontbestand* includes Army aircraft only; there is no equivalent inventory for Naval aircraft.

The *Frontbestand* is a combination of Prussian and Bavarian inventory reports submitted to the air staffs monthly. Although several of the Bavarian reports exist, most of the original reports were

apparently destroyed when the War Archive in Potsdam was bombed in WW2. Unfortunately, the data that has survived, which is from Hoff's 1920 article, is only the data for every other month. Thus the resolution of the information is 60 days, not the 30 provided by the original momthly data, now lost. Regrettably, most of the data for October 31, 1918, is missing, probably due to the desperate German military situation 11 days before the armistice.

The data in the *Frontbestand* tables is raw data. That is important to keep in mind because some of it is in error for various reasons that require some discussion. Known information is given in the relevant section. Regardless, there are unanswered questions.

Aircraft Type Designations

Idflieg required manufacturers to build better designs from other manufacturers under license. At first an aircraft built under license was given a completely new type designation! For example, the DFW C.V built under license was also designated the Halberstadt C.I, Aviatik C.IV, and LVG C.VI. That was a very confusing system, and in late 1916 *Idflieg* rationalized the designation system to accurately

Amazingly, aircraft built under license by a different manufacturer initially were given a completely new type designation! This has been the cause of great confusion and must be kept in mind when using the *Frontbestand* tables. *Idflieg* changed the system to reflect both the original design and the license manufacturer. At left is a list of the new designations based on the original design and the old based on the license manufacturer, together with the earliest known time of the change in designations.

Designations of License-Built Aircraft		
New Designation	**Old Designation**	**Usage**
Ago C.IV(Rat)	Rathgeber C.I	In use 8 Oct. 1917
Albatros B.II(Bay)	BFW B.II	?
Albatros B.II(Mer)	Mercur B.II	Changed 14 Feb. 1917
Albatros B.III(Bay)	BFW B.II	In use 13 Dec. 1916
Albatros C.I(Rol)	Roland C.I	In use 19 Dec. 1916
Albatros C.Ia(Bay)	BFW C.I	In use 18 Dec. 1916
Albatros C.III(Bay)	BFW C.I	In use 15 Sep. 1916
Albatros C.VII(Bay)	BFW C.II	In use 15 Sep. 1916
Albatros D.II(LVG)	LVG D.I	?
Aviatik C.I(Han)	Hannover C.I	In use 15 Sep. 1916
DFW C.V(Av)	Aviatik C.IV	In use 20 Dec. 1916
DFW C.V(Halb)	Halberstadt C.I	Changed 9 Feb. 1917
DFW C.V(Halb)	Halberstadt C.IV	?
DFW C.V(LVG)	LVG C.VI	Changed 28 Mar. 1917
Friedrichshafen G.II(Daim)	Daimler G.II	In use 16 Nov. 1916
Halberstadt D.II(Av)	Aviatik D.I	In use 19 Sep. 1916
Halberstadt D.II(Han)	Hannover D.I	In use 19 Sep. 1916
Roland C.IIa(Li)	Linke-Hofmann C.I	In use 13 Dec. 1916
Roland D.I(Pfal)	Pfalz D.I	In use 13 Jan. 1917
Roland D.II(Pfal)	Pfalz D.II	In use 13 Jan. 1917
Rumpler C.Ia(Han)	Hannover C.II	Changed 10 Jan. 1917
Rumpler C.IV(Pfal)	Pfalz C.I	In use 16 Nov. 1916
Rumpler C.IV(Pfal)	Pfalz C.IV	?

Left: The SSW D.VI was not completed until after the armistice; by then the 'E' category for monoplane fighters was no longer used. Powered by the 220 hp Sh.IIIa high-altitude counter-rotary engine, it had a top speed of 220 kmh (137 mph) coupled with excellent maneuverability and climb and a ceiling of 8,000m. The under-fuselage fuel tank was jettisonable in case of fire. It was the natural production successor to the SSW D.IV.

Above: The DFW C.V was the best second-generation C-type general-purpose two-seater. Powered by the 200 hp Benz Bz.IV, more DFW C.Vs were built (3,955) than any other German warplane, and it served in large numbers until the armistice. The DFW C.V above built by Aviatik under license was initially known as the Aviatik C.IV before being re-designated the DFW C.V(Av) as seen painted on the nose. DFW C.Vs built by Halberstadt were initially known as the Halberstadt C.I or C.IV before being re-designated the DFW C.V(Halb), and those built by LVG initially were known as the LVG C.VI before being re-designated the DFW C.V(LVG). The DFW C.V was hardly unique in this respect; other widely-used aircraft built under license by other manufacturers suffered from the same problem until the system was changed in late 1916.

reflect the original design and license manufacturer. However, the old designations crept into military records and lingered on in Bavarian reports as late as December 1917.

The adjacent table of old and new designations, taken from original records, demonstrates the clarity of the new system compared to the old, and must be taken into account when using the *Frontbestand* tables.

On an individual aircraft, the type designation was followed by the serial number of the aircraft. The serial number had a slash followed by the last two digits of the year the purchase was approved. There could be a delay between the time the purchase was approved and the contract was signed; for example, a contact signed in January of one year could still specify a range of serial numbers with the prior year suffix if the purchase was approved in the prior year.

Below: Twenty massive Lubeck-Travemünde F2 reconnaissance floatplanes were used on over-water missions by the Navy. It was powered by the rare 220 hp Mercedes D.IV straight-eight, created by the expedient of adding two more cylinders to the D.III six-cylinder engine.

Early Unarmed Aircraft

Miscellaneous Types

Germany started the war with a mixed collection of aircraft, mostly two-seaters, for reconnaissance. In the miscellaneous category, the DFW Mars could be either the A/13 monoplane or the B/13 biplane. The Farman was likely an airplane impressed into service at the start of the war. The Parasol listed here could only be the Pfalz A.I or A.II parasols and should be included with those entries in the A-class *Frontbestand* table.

A-Types

Class A aircraft were unarmed monoplanes, both one and two seat. Most A-types were the *Taube* configuration, but there were also Fokker and Pfalz A-types.

During the early period in which A-types were active, there was little uniformity in aircraft designations, and different units reported the same aircraft type in different ways. In August 1915, *Idflieg* promulgated a more standardized aircraft type designation system, and the aircraft type was now followed by a Roman numeral to signify the

sequence of the design. For example, Pfalz A.II signifies the second unarmed monoplane design (A-type) by the Pfalz company. This new designation was applied retroactively. Unfortunately, the key to the retroactive numbering of the Roman class number is missing, leading to some ambiguity.

From actual factory records, it is known that Gotha built A-type aircraft in 1913 and 1914 but none in 1915. So the aircraft designated Gotha A.I must have come from the A/13 and A/14 production. The *Frontbestand* table shows three rows for the Gotha A/13, A/14, and A.I; these three rows were all the same aircraft type and should be combined to show just the Gotha A.I. The Gotha *Taube* A-type lasted longer than other *Taube* at the front because it was the best *Taube* of all.

Similarly, the Fokker A. and A/14 remain unidentified, but were one of three types; the Fokker A.I (also known as the M 8), Fokker A.II ((also known as the M 5L), and Fokker A.III (also known as the M 5K) (type identification from the *Geschichte der Deutschen Flugzeugindustrie*, *Idflieg*, Berlin, 1918,

Above & Right: The DFW *Mars,* produced in both monoplane and biplane variants, was one of the miscellaneous primitive types with which Germany entered the war.

Above: Gotha *Taube*, the best and longest-lived of the *Taube* types.
Right: *Taube* used by the German garrison in China. The inherently stable *Tauben* were too stable for air combat and their great drag limited performance. *Tauben* soon disappeared from the front, replaced by higher-performance biplanes.

Frontbeststand Inventory of Miscellaneous Aircraft at the Front

Manufacturer and Type	1914			1915						1916						1917						1918			
	31 Aug	31 Oct	31 Dec	28 Feb	30 Apr	30 Jun	31 Aug	31 Oct	31 Dec	28 Feb	30 Apr	30 Jun	31 Aug	31 Oct	31 Dec	28 Feb	30 Apr	30 Jun	31 Aug	31 Oct	31 Dec	28 Feb	30 Apr	30 Jun	31 Aug
Brandenburg		3																							
DFW Mars	1	2		5																					
Farman		1																							
Parasol			1	1	5	17	18	15		2	1														
Total:	1	6	1	6	5	17	18	15		2	1														

Frontbeststand Inventory of A-Type Aircraft (Un-Armed Two-Seat Monoplanes) at the Front

Manufacturer	Type	1914			1915						1916						1917						1918			
		31 Aug	31 Oct	31 Dec	28 Feb	30 Apr	30 Jun	31 Aug	31 Oct	31 Dec	28 Feb	30 Apr	30 Jun	31 Aug	31 Oct	31 Dec	28 Feb	30 Apr	30 Jun	31 Aug	31 Oct	31 Dec	28 Feb	30 Apr	30 Jun	31 Aug
Albatros	A/13	5		1			2																			
	A/14			1		1	8																			
	A.		2	5	7	8																				
	A.I	2						2	2																	
	A.II							2																		
Fokker	A/14			2				1		2	1															
	A.		5	1	15																					
	A.I			6	8	7	10	2	3	2	1	1														
	A.II					13	4	4	4	4	3	2														
	A.III					1	3	1	2		2	2														
Gotha	A/13	13	3	6	2	15																				
	A/14	3	5	14	4	2	4				2	2	1													
	A.I		5	4			1		2																	
Halberstadt	A.II			2	5	5	3																			
Hirth	A.	1																								
Jeannin	A/13	6																								
	A/14	3	9	7	16	3	1																			
Kondor	A/13			1																						
	A/14		1	3	6	1																				
LVG	A.	1																								
	A/14						1																			
Otto	A.		2																							
Parasol	A.			1	2																					
	A.I							1																		
Pfalz	A.I								3																	
	A.II																	1								
	A/15									1	1															
Rumpler	A/13	2																								
	A/14	8	3																							
Total:		44	36	53	65	56	37	13	16	13	10	7	2													

Note: There are some errors in the *Frontbeststand* tables; these are discussed in the appropriate sections.
Left: The Pfalz Parasol was redesignated Pfalz A.I or A.II, depending on engine, in August 1915; this one is from *Flieger-Abteilung* 3b. *Leutnant* Hempel at left was the pilot; *Oberleutnant* Erhard Ergener at right was the observer. Hempel used the cloth tucked into a button hole on his flight suit to wipe engine oil from his flight goggles, a necessity for rotary-engine aircraft.

This Pfalz Parasol, later designated Pfalz A.I, was assigned to *Flieger Abteilung* 9b in July 1915 and engaged in missions against Italy in the Alps despite the fact that Italy and Germany were not then at war! The red/white bands, the Austro-Hungarian colors, were to make the Italian think the aircraft was Austro-Hungarian. The crew was *Lt.* Marz and *Lt.* Wissel.

Above: This unarmed Fokker M8 was later redesignated the Fokker A.I. Power was an 80 hp Oberursel U.0 7-cylinder rotary.

Left: The Albatros *Taube* was retroactively designated the Albatros A. The *Taube* configuration inherently had a great deal of drag, limiting speed and climb, and the *Taube* soon disappeared from front-line units, replaced by higher-performance biplanes that were not as stable but had the better maneuverability, climb, and speed found to be necessary in combat operations.

p.129). For *Frontbestand* purposes, the Fokker A. and A/14 data should have been combined.

Likewise, the Parasol A. and A.I are identical with the Pfalz A.I and these three rows of data should be combined. The Pfalz A.II and A/15 are probably the same type.

The Halberstadt A.II was a Fokker M 8 built under license. Nothing is known of the Hirth A, LVG A., LVG A/14, and Otto A. Finally, *FFA* 14 was reported to have three Rumpler *Taube* on strength in February 1915, but they are not listed in the table.

B-Types

Unarmed two-seat biplanes were retroactively designated 'B' types. The A-type monoplanes had limited performance and most had faded from the inventory by the end of 1915; only two remained in the inventory by the end of June 1916.

The B-type biplanes were more rugged and offered better performance than the A-types, so lasted longer at the front. Built by a variety of companies, B-types were numerous into the spring of 1916 and a few were still in front-line service, perhaps for training and liaison, until the end of the war. Beginning in mid-1915 they were gradually replaced at the front by armed two-seaters; these early C-types were often developments of B-types.

B-types remained in production until the armistice for training aircraft. For example, in 1917 alone more than 3,000 B-types were ordered as trainers. After February 1916, those B-types that show up in the *Frontbestand* table were trainers used behind the front, communication machines, and unit hacks. The large numbers of B-types used for training in Germany do not appear in the *Frontbestand*.

At this time there is no way to know what specific aircraft are represented by the B/12, B/12, and B. of Aviatik, Albatros, Euler, LVG, and

Otto. The 'B Lf' listed under Albatros was a Navy *Landflugzeug* (land aircraft); it may have been attached to an Army unit or vice versa, but the reason it is listed in unknown.

The sudden appearance of 100 Albatros B/13 in June 1915 is a mystery. It could be a typographical error and probably should have been counted as Albatros B.II aircraft.

Similarly, the entry of 35 Fokker B.I in April 1916 is a mystery and almost certainly an error; the type was long out of production.

The LVG B.III prototype did not appear until November 1917, so the listing of 6 of these in December 1915 must be an error.

The Roland B.I was the Albatros B.II built under license by Roland and later designated Albatros B.II(Rol). These aircraft should have been included in the Albatros B.II numbers in the *Frontbestand*, which included aircraft built under license by other manufacturers.

The Otto B/14, B.I, and B. are difficult to identify, but the B/14 and B. probably represent the Otto Pusher used by the Bavarian Army in 1913–1914; some were still in service in 1915. The Otto B.I in August 1915 was probably the LVG B-type built under license and should have been included in those numbers.

Above: LVG B.I in Bavarian service at the front.

Frontbeststand Inventory of B-Type Aircraft (Un-Armed Two-Seat Biplanes) at the Front

Manufacturer and Type		1914 31 Aug	1914 31 Oct	1914 31 Dec	1915 28 Feb	1915 30 Apr	1915 30 Jun	1915 31 Aug	1915 31 Oct	1915 31 Dec	1916 28 Feb	1916 30 Apr	1916 30 Jun	1916 31 Aug	1916 31 Oct	1916 31 Dec	1917 28 Feb	1917 30 Apr	1917 30 Jun	1917 31 Aug	1917 31 Oct	1917 31 Dec	1918 28 Feb	1918 30 Apr	1918 30 Jun	1918 31 Aug
AEG	B.I	3	2	3	8	1	2		1	2							1									
	B.II					8	8	9																		
Albatros	B/12	1																								
	B/13	6	3	7	3		100	2																		
	B.		2	3	41	55																				
	B.I	18	27	55	87	157	145	116	90	42	26	7	3	3	5	1				1	1	2				
	B.II	5	9	7	14	27	30	149	212	185	92	49	30	5	6	12	3	5	4	3	3	2	3	3	7	5
	B.IIa																						1	1		4
	B Lf																	1	1							
Aviatik	B/12	1																								
	B/13	34	24	13	4	4	2	1	1			1	1							1						
	B.				17	23																				
	B.I	12	43	51	28	53	48	35	20	11		5														
	B.II						1	29	38	32	18	7	2			1										
	B.III										2															
Brandenburg	B.I			2	1																					
	B.II				1																					
DFW	B.I	2	17	12	2			1																		
Euler	B/13	2																								
	B.I	3	1	2				3			1	1														
	B.II							5																		
Fokker	B/13	1																								
	B.I				1	3	12	4	4		1	35														
Gotha	B.I		1				1			5		3														
Halberstadt	B.I						2	3	4	2	1									1						
	B.II							3	3	8	2	5	3													
	B.III								5	6	2	5	3													
	B.																1	1								
LVG	B.	22	17	22	62	65	15																			
	B/13	30	14	13	1	3	9	7	2		2															
	B.I	32	42	60	61	106	124	94	37	14	7	6	4			4										
	B.II			12	16	31	52	95	165	77	40	16	10	5	3	2										
	B.III									6																
Otto	B/14					1																				
	B.I		1					8																		
	B.					3																				
Roland	B.I											32					4	1								
Rumpler	B.I	1	6	21	32	41	38	17	14	6	5	4	2	8												
Unidentified																	1									
Total:		173	209	283	379	581	589	580	597	396	198	176	60	13	22	21	9	9	7	5	4	4	4	4	7	9

Right: The Albatros B.I was a typical early, unarmed two-seat reconnaissance airplane. Powered by a 100 hp Mercedes D.I, it had good flying qualities and was later used for training.

Albatros B.I named *Weddigen* serving with *Feld-Flieger Abteilung* 2.

LVG B.I(Ot) 636/16. The serial number suffix '16', indicating its order was approved in 1916, and white outline around the national insignia are characteristic of use as a trainer. By 1916 B-types were purchased for training, not front-line use. Aircraft used for training in Germany were not counted in the *Frontbestand*.

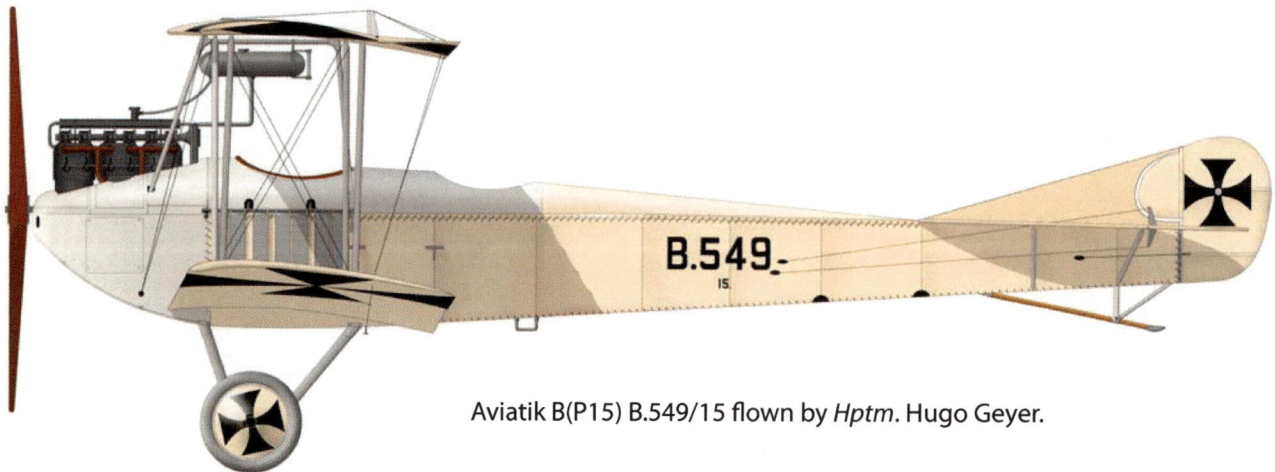

Aviatik B(P15) B.549/15 flown by *Hptm*. Hugo Geyer.

Most early aircraft were in plain finish of clear-doped linen with the early version of the iron cross national insignia. In many cases the insignia was painted directly on the fabric, while in others it was painted on a white background for contrast. Later the white background was reduced to a 50mm white outline.

Above: This Otto B-type pusher built under license by Pfalz was flown by Bruno Büchner in German East Afrika and is being protected by Askari troops. A large tropical radiator is installed under the upper wing center section and a primitive bomb-dropping chute has been attached to the side of the nacelle. In contrast to the Allies, who produced pusher aircraft in great quantity, Germany manufactured few pusher designs.

Above: A typical Aviatik B-type is readied for a reconnaissance mission early in the war. The pilot, Herman Göring, would later become a leading fighter ace and win the *Pour le Mérite*. Unfortunately, he also became a notorius Nazi leader post-war.

Armed Two-Seat Aircraft

C Types

At the beginning of the war there was essentially no air-to-air combat and aircraft could go about their duties unarmed. But by the spring of 1915 that changed as more pilots began attacking one another in the air. *Idflieg* had been considering the problem of air-to-air combat, and decided to procure armed two-seat biplanes, a category to which they gave the designation **C-type**. Many of these new C-types were simple developments of their respective manufacturers' earlier B-types. Generally the first generation C-types had an engine of 150 to 160 horsepower and a flexible machine gun for the observer. Apparatus to synchronize a machine gun to fire between the blades of a rotating propeller was developed in mid-1915, and soon a fixed, synchronized gun for the pilot was added, creating the standard armament configuration for armed two-seaters for the rest of the war.

When the 200 hp Benz became available, it was installed in a new generation of C-types starting with the DFW C.V, Aviatik C.II, and Rumpler C.III.

Greater power increased the payload and improved the speed, climb, and ceiling of these aircraft. The DFW C.V was so successful that it was purchased in greater numbers than any other German aircraft and served in large numbers until the end of the war.

The armed two-seater was the most versatile aircraft type and performed the most important battle-field tasks. As the war ground on, new tactics and battlefield roles were developed and new classes of two-seaters were developed to perform them.

Around the same time the 200 hp Benz appeared the 220 hp Mercedes D.IV straight-eight engine also became available by the simple expedient of adding two more cylinders to the six-cylinder 160 hp Mercedes D.III engine. This new engine was used in small numbers in two new high-speed (for the time) reconnaissance aircraft, the Albatros C.V and LVG. C.IV. When these aircraft reached the Front both were as fast as contemporary Allied fighters. Despite their more specialized nature, they were still designated C-types.

Above: The Aviatik C.I, developed from the earlier Aviatik B.II, and powered by engines of 150–160 hp, was one of the most numerous early C-types. At the dawn of air combat it was not yet certain that the gunner should be in the rear cockpit for a better field of fire to defend against attacking fighters, and *Idflieg* directed Aviatik to retain the observer in the forward cockpit for better visibility forward and downward. A gun was mounted on each of the two rails alongside the front cockpit for the observer's use.

Frontbeststand Inventory of C-Type Aircraft (Armed Two-Seat Biplanes) at the Front

Manufacturer	Type	1914 31 Aug	1914 31 Oct	1914 31 Dec	1915 28 Feb	1915 30 Apr	1915 30 Jun	1915 31 Aug	1915 31 Oct	1915 31 Dec	1916 28 Feb	1916 30 Apr	1916 30 Jun	1916 31 Aug	1916 31 Oct	1916 31 Dec	1917 28 Feb	1917 30 Apr	1917 30 Jun	1917 31 Aug	1917 31 Oct	1917 31 Dec	1918 28 Feb	1918 30 Apr	1918 30 Jun	1918 31 Aug
AEG	C.I						4	10	28	26	34	34		1	1	1	1	1								
	C.II											1														
	C.IV								1						9	42	90	124	127	63	88	68	40	26	29	34
Ago	C.I						5	5	9	14	22	15	23	16	9	8	5	1								
	C.II									2	1															
	C.III										1															
	C.IV															8	25	1	19	90	42	13	3			
Albatros	C (Hirth)			1																						
	C.I				1		36	91	184	278	349	213	165	143	125	90	52	37	46	13	4	2		1	1	1
	C.III									12	51	208	300	354	320	320	214	174	107	29	15	5	1	1	2	
	C.IV												1				1	2		2						
	C.V													65	57	47	50	60	57	29	8	5	5			
	C.VI													8	71	53	111	21	3	1						
	C.VII												2		94	249	372	296	165	74	33	11	6	4		1
	C.VIII																	1	1	1	1		1	1		
	C.IX																		2	2	1	1	1	1		
	C.X															2		70	98	47	26	11	4			
	C.XII																		41	93	92	66	48	36	20	15
	C Lf																3	1								
Aviatik	C.I				1		8	9	35	81	161	150	219	183	177	110	63	27	12	1	1					
	C.II								3		7	6				22	62	50	34	4	1					
	C.III													26	47	22	20	6	2							
	C.V																		1							
DFW	C.I									25		2	2	9	6		5	3	1	1						
	C.V													21		42	79	341	839	1057	901	845	614	665	623	620
Gotha	C.I								2																	
Halberstadt	C.I																	4								
	C.V																	3							10	192
	C.IV																		15	65				40		
	C (exp.)																					1				
Hannover	C.I																	2								
	C.II																			19						
LVG	C.I						30	60	35	45	25	11	4	5	1	1		1								
	C.II						8	6	20	138	214	249	255	220	195	155	87	45	20	8	2	3				
	C.IV									1	1	1		27	60	76	58	39	14	1						
	C.V																			98	219	446	504	565	312	133
	C.VI																								173	400
Otto	C.I			1					1	9	1	1														
Pfalz	C.I			2																	3	24	11	7	9	6
	C.IV																	2								
Roland	C.I												35				21	9	1							
	C.II											17	35	37	45	40	53	42	1	1						
	C.IIa													13	11	24			12	1						
	C.III																1									
Rumpler	C.I									29	67	120	144	202	231	190	145	107	55	37	40	16	11	9	5	4
	C.Ia															2	1	52	162	129	30	5	3	3	2	1
	C.III															1	42	22	15	7	1	1	1	1		
	C.IV																	24	122	257	225	208	161	187	182	110
	C.V																				3	9			4	6
	C.VII																					17	48	94	112	85
	C.IX																					20	13	11	5	2
Unidentified																						20				
Total:				4	2		91	181	318	660	934	1029	1184	1302	1487	1508	1561	1557	1966	2061	1821	1797	1475	1611	1528	1610

Above: The Aviatik C.II, developed from the C.I, used the more powerful 200 hp Benz Bz.IV engine, making it faster than the C.I. Unfortunately, at *Idflieg's* insistence it retained the observer in the front cockpit and the side-mounted guns, making for a cramped working envirnment and restricted field of fire. Unusual for a two-seater, the pilot had a headrest! Only a single production batch of 75 Aviatik C.IIs was constructed, after which Aviatik was directed to produce the DFW C.V under license. The Aviatik C.II and DFW C.V used the same engine and construction techniques, so had similar speed. However, the DFW had excellent maneuverability and handling qualities, critical attributes the Aviatik C.II lacked.

However, from this time, the evolution of the two-seat warplane branched into a number of paths as combat roles expanded and grew more specialized. For the typical general-purpose artillery spotting and short-range reconnaissance tasks, newer airframes using the 200 hp Benz Bz.IV and its derivatives were developed. The Albatros C.VII, LVG C.V, LVG C.VI, and Halberstadt C.V were production aircraft in this branch of development. A foray into using the more powerful 260 hp Mercedes in the general-purpose Albatros C.X and C.XII met with limited success. These aircraft, developed from the earlier, successful Albatros C.VII, were elegant-looking aircraft of mediocre performance for their time.

From mid-March to mid-May 1918 a C-type competition was held at Adlershof to choose the new C-types to go into production. This was done based on the successful example of the first fighter competition that had taken place at the beginning of 1918 and resulted in delivery of better fighters. The C-type armed two-seat biplanes were the largest proportion of warplanes built during the war, reflecting the great importance of their work.

License-built types are included in the C-type

Frontbestand with few exceptions. There are some anomalies in the December 1914 C-type *Frontbestand*, because there were no C-type machines at that time. The Albatros C(Hirth) is unidentified; it may be one of the competition machines flown by Hellmuth Hirth before being impressed, or possibly the first C-type designed by him. The Otto C.I and Pfalz C.I entries are unexplained and must be errors. Nor was there a Gotha C.I; Gotha production charts confirm Gotha never built a C.I. Was this perhaps a Gotha B-type modified with a machine gun?

The Albatros 'C Lf" was a German Navy C-type landplane; perhaps these were attached to Army units?

The Halberstadt C.I and C.V listings for June 1917 and C.IV listings in late 1917 are errors directly attributable to the confusion of designations of license-built aircraft. The Halberstadt C.I and C.IV were actually the DFW C.V built by Halberstadt under license, as was the Halberstadt C.V listed for June 1917. The true Halberstadt C.V was an original Halberstadt design that entered service in June 1918 as shown correctly in the table.

Flz.Bild-A.10567

Above: This DFW C.V was built under license by Aviatik. Although the observer was in the rear cockpit with a better field of fire than the Aviatik C.II, the C.II could easily have been modified to the observer in back configuration. However, the modified C.II would not have matched the DFW's excellent maneuverability and handling. A total of 3,955 DFW C.Vs were built, more than any other WW1 German warplane. Of that total, Aviatik built 1,400 machines to 12 production orders.

Right: The Albatros C.III, powered by the 150 hp Benz or 160 hp Mercedes, was one of the best and most widely-used first generation C-types. Availability of the 200 hp Benz resulted in the second generation of C-types like the Aviatik C.II, Albatros C.VII, and the best of that generation, the DFW C.V.

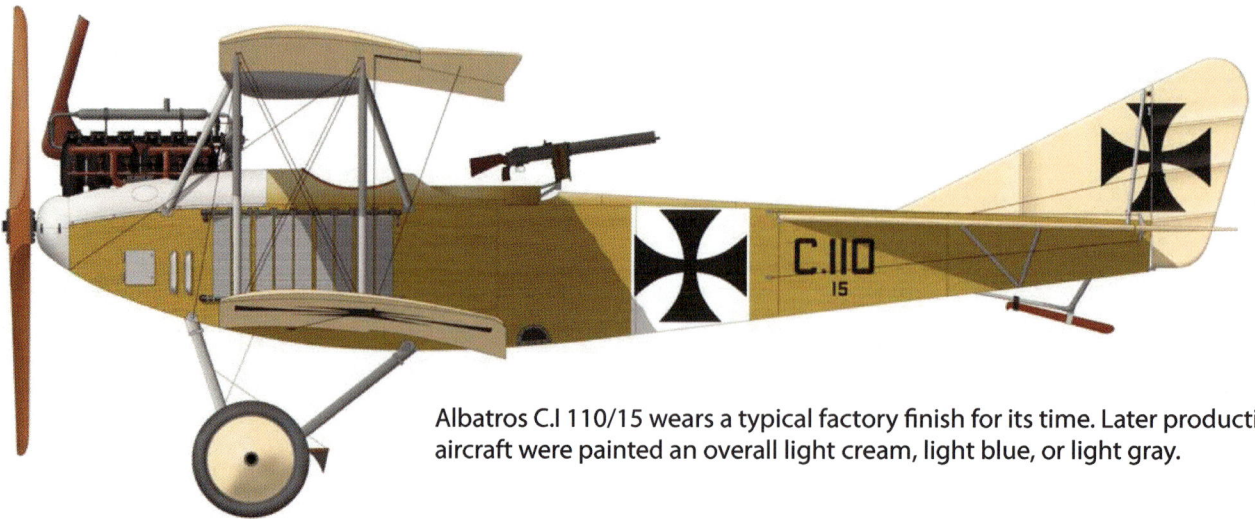

Albatros C.I 110/15 wears a typical factory finish for its time. Later production aircraft were painted an overall light cream, light blue, or light gray.

This Albatros C.III is in factory finish with simple tactical markings added in black. It was flown by *Lt*. Gerhard Bassenge and *Vzfw*. Ernst Floel of *Kasta* 39 during late 1916.

This early Roland C.II is in typical early factory finish with an early shark mouth and eyes and the name *Meerkatze* on the aft fuselage. Like other early Roland C.II aircraft, it lacked a synchronized gun for the pilot.

Above: The Roland C.II, used in small numbers, was for a time the best German warplane at the front. Much faster than contemporary German C-types due to its streamlining, it was also faster than Allied fighters when it first reached the front. Early models lacked a gun for the pilot, but once this was provided, as shown here, the C.II *Walfisch* (Whale) became a two-seat fighter, presaging the later CL-category aircraft. It used the 160 hp Mercedes D.III engine.

Left: The Otto C.I was one of the few German pusher designs to reach operations. In contrast, the Allies used the pusher configuration extensively. The advantage of the pusher was a large forward field of view for the observer, who was normally seated in front. But pushers had a major blind spot aft, which made them more vulnerable to enemy fighters, and their high drag made them slow.

Right: The Ago C.I was another of the few German pusher designs and was used in small numbers.

Above: Powered by the rare 220 hp Mercedes D.IV straight-eight engine, the LVG C.IV was faster than Allied fighters when it first reached the front. Due to its speed it was used primarily for photo-reconnaissance. *Britenschreck* sports a shark face. Although individual markings were more common on fighters, they were often seen on two-seaters.

Above: The Ago C.IV was one of the unusual two-seaters to reach operations. The forward inner interplane strut was omitted to give the gunner a better field of fire forward, and unlike most airplanes of the time the wings were tapered. Power was the 200 hp Benz Bz.IV engine.

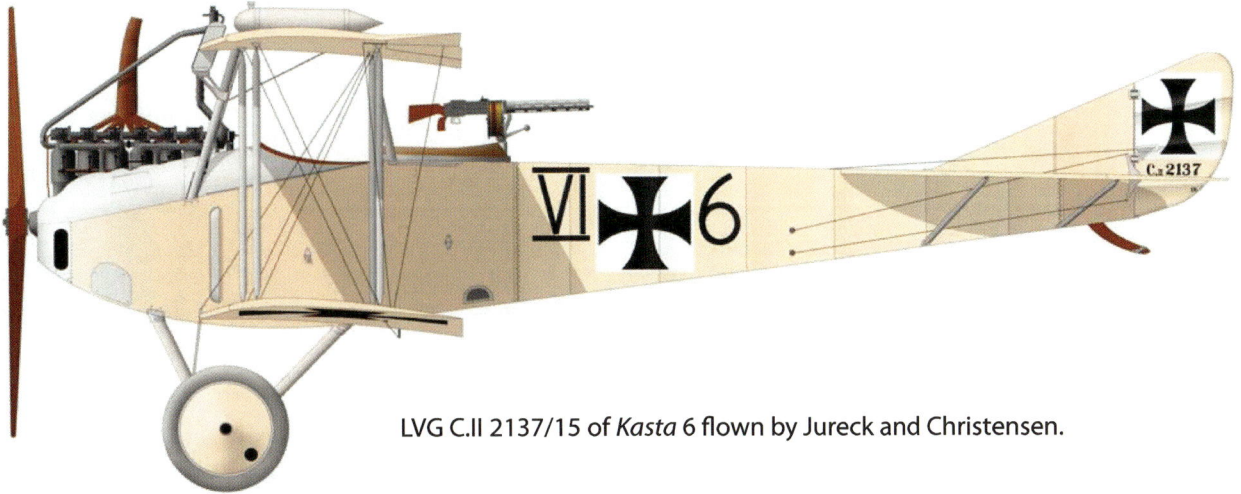

LVG C.II 2137/15 of *Kasta* 6 flown by Jureck and Christensen.

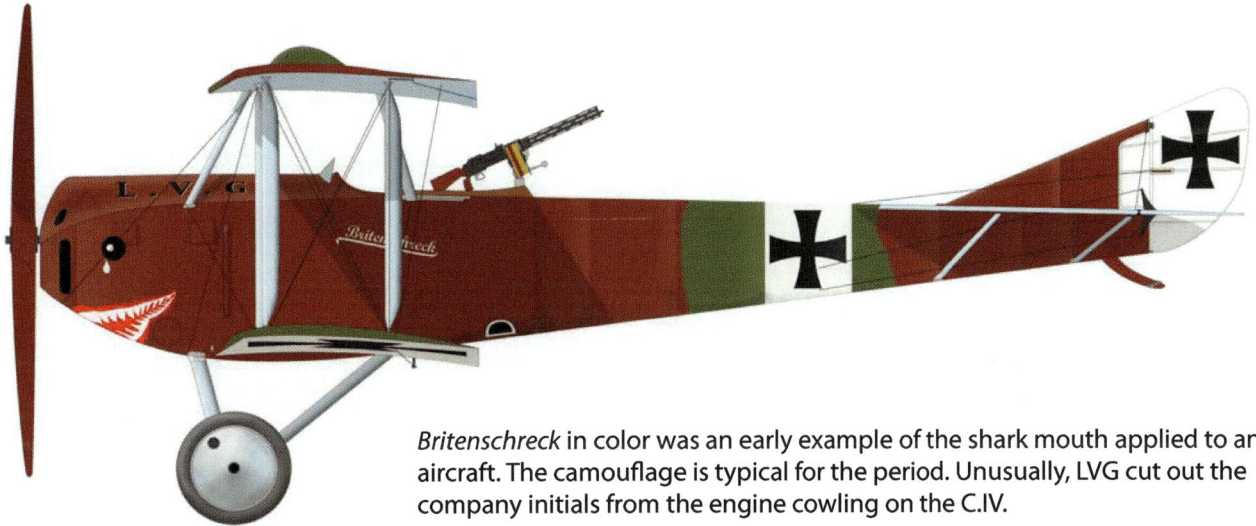

Britenschreck in color was an early example of the shark mouth applied to an aircraft. The camouflage is typical for the period. Unusually, LVG cut out the company initials from the engine cowling on the C.IV.

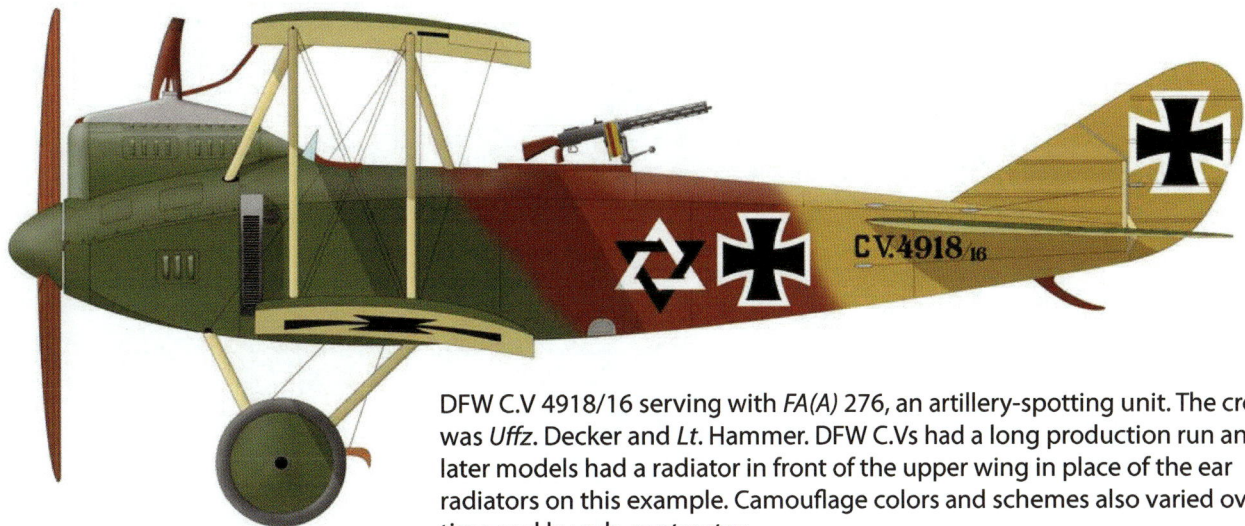

DFW C.V 4918/16 serving with *FA(A)* 276, an artillery-spotting unit. The crew was *Uffz*. Decker and *Lt*. Hammer. DFW C.Vs had a long production run and later models had a radiator in front of the upper wing in place of the ear radiators on this example. Camouflage colors and schemes also varied over time and by sub-contractor.

Above: Like the LVG C.IV the Albatros C.V was powered by the rare 220 hp Mercedes D.IV straight-eight engine and was faster than Allied fighters when it first reached the front. Due to its speed it was used primarily for photo-reconnaissance. The geared engine was completely enclosed by the cowling, assisting streamlining, and the low propeller speed allowed a large, efficient propeller to be fitted.
Below: The Albatros C.VII, powered by the 200 hp Benz Bz.IV engine, was a successful general reconnaissance airplane. Using an airframe similar to the C.V, it is easily distinguished by its engine protruding above the cowling.

Right: Powered by the 260 hp Mercedes D.IVa six-cylinder engine, the Albatros C.X was an enlarged C.VII. The C.X had mediocre performance for its time and most were used on the Eastern Front where fighter opposition was much less severe than the Western Front.

Left: Powered by the 260 hp Mercedes D.IVa six-cylinder engine, the Albatros C.XII was a more streamlined C.X. Like the C.X, the C.XII had mediocre performance for its time despite its elegance and most were used on the less demanding Eastern Front.

Above & Above Right: After the disappointing C.X and C.XII, Albatros turned to a smaller design. A single C.XIV was produced, and after some modifications it went into production as the Albatros C.XV. Powered by a 220 hp Benz BZ.IVa six-cylinder engine, the Albatros C.XV was faster and more maneuverable than its larger predecessors. In production at the end of the war, it is not certain it reached operations; however, it enjoyed an extensive postwar career.

Albatros C.VII 1330/16 of *Flieger Abteilung 7*. The white arrow is the unit marking. Unusually, a radiator has been mounted in front of the wing, probably a modification carried out at the unit. C.VIIs normally had 'ear' radiators on the sides of the fuselage. A captured Lewis gun is mounted over the wing center section to supplement the standard fixed fun for the pilot.

This Albatros C.X is in the standard factory finish. Not visible in this side view, the upper surfaces of the wings and tailplane normally had a two-color or three-color sprayed camouflage scheme depending on sub-contractor.

This C.XII carries a lightning bolt unit marking over its standard factory finish. This aircraft was flown by *Lt.* Geiger and *Lt.* Rein in June 1917. Like the C.X, the upper wings and tailplane were normally sprayed in a two-color or three-color camouflage scheme.

Above: Tired of paying royalties on the DFW C.V it was building under license, LVG hired its designer and the LVG C.V was a refinement of the DFW C.V. **Left:** The LVG C.VI was a more compact derivative of the LVG C.VI. Both C.V and C.VI were tough, maneuverable, widely used reconnaissance airplanes. **Below:** The handsome LVG C.VIII prototype was too late to see operational service.

This LVG C.V of *Schusta* 11 in October 1917 displays black and white fuselage unit markings over the standard factory finish. The upper wings and tail surfaces were sprayed in camouflage colors.

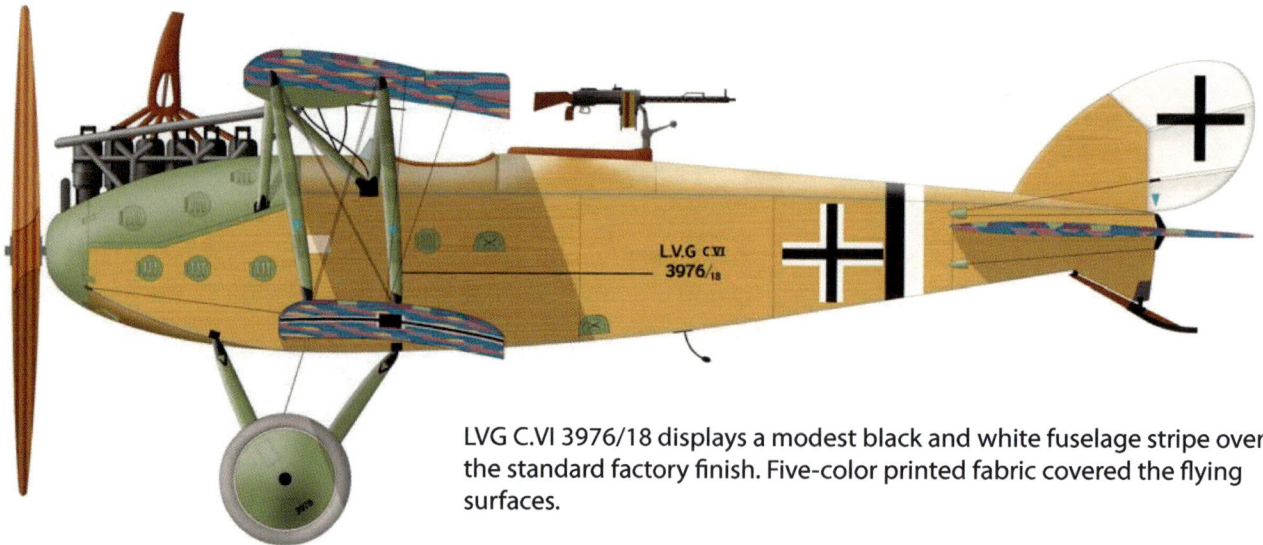

LVG C.VI 3976/18 displays a modest black and white fuselage stripe over the standard factory finish. Five-color printed fabric covered the flying surfaces.

Halberstadt C.V(DFW) 4185/18; DFW-built C.Vs were painted in a light gray with five-color printed fabric covering their flying surfaces.

Above: The Aviatik C.III was an extensively-streamlined development of the C.I to improve its speed. Using the same 160 hp Mercedes D.III engine as the C.I, the C.III was 35 km/h faster; in fact, it was as fast as the C.II powered by the 200 hp Benz. Being so closely related to the C.I and using the same engine, the C.III actually reached the front before the C.II. Like the C.I and C.II, the C.III seated the observer in front, where his side-mounted guns had limited fields of fire. Unlike the C.II, the C.III possessed excellent handling qualities, so much so that late in the war 200 were ordered for use as trainers.

Above: Early production models of the Rumpler C.I were powered by the 160 hp Mercedes D.III, and immediately established themselves as reliable airplanes with good performance and handling qualities. Some later production C.Is had a 150 hp Benz Bz.III or 180 hp Argus As.III. The C.I was an excellent general purpose C-type that was popular with its crews.

Above: Powered by the 200 hp Benz Bz.IV six-cylinder engine, the prototype Rumpler C.III shows its elegant lines. The streamlined fairing behind the observer was replaced by a simple rounded deck on production machines, which likely improved the observer's field of fire. Initial production C.III aircraft retained the fragile rudder without fixed fin, but operational experience demonstrated the need for more stability and a fixed fin was added. Constant development of the airframe, especially the control surfaces, resulted in the late-production C.III being virtually indistinguishable from the early production C.IV except for its engine. The C.III abandoned the C.I airframe, with its excellent flying qualities, in search of significantly improved high-altitude performance, but the 200 hp Benz could not provide it. The basic airframe did not reach its potential until the 260 hp Mercedes D.IVa was installed to create the C.IV.

Above: Powered by the 260 hp Mercedes D.IVa six-cylinder engine, the graceful Rumpler C.IV was as fast as Allied fighters at its ceiling, were few fighters could reach it. It became the premier German long-range photo-reconnaissance airplane. Over-compressed engines designed for more power at higher altitude maintained its edge throughout the war. The Rumpler C.IV airframe was also used for the specialized *lichtbild* (photo) aircraft.

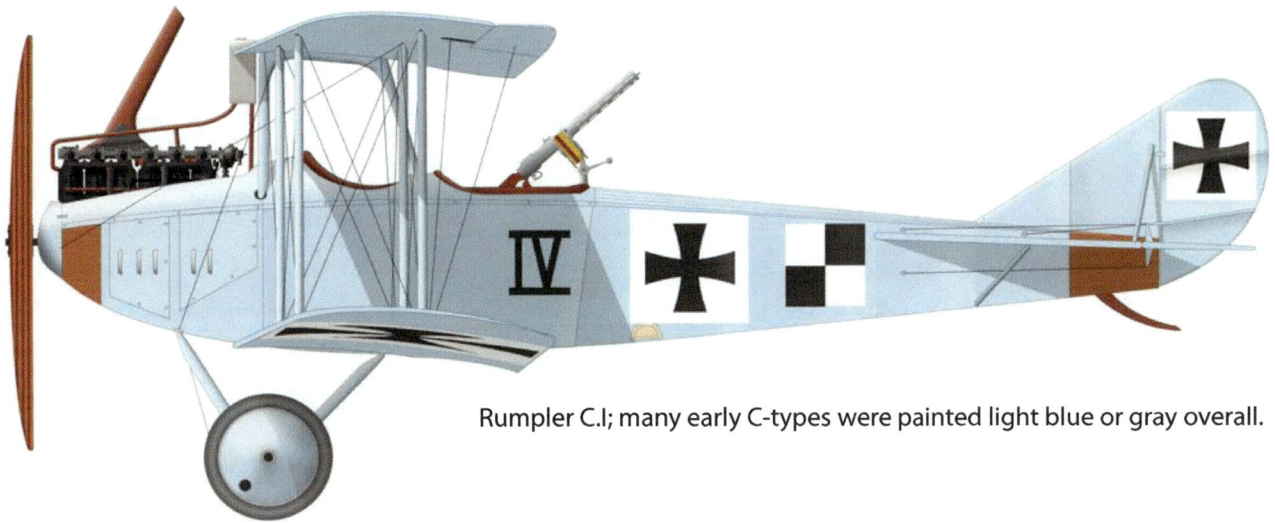

Rumpler C.I; many early C-types were painted light blue or gray overall.

This Rumpler C.IV is a later-production model without propeller spinner. It wears standard factory camouflage enhanced with red/ white/black (German national colors) markings on the fuselage, wheel covers, wing struts, and nose, making it more colorful than most Rumplers.

The Fokker V.38, prototype for the Fokker C.I two-seat fighter, was covered in printed camouflage fabric overall with natural metal panels, Fokker's standard factory finish late in the war.

Left: Powered by a 185 hp BMW.IIIa, the Fokker V38 was the prototype Fokker C.I , which was too late for combat but served postwar. Essentially it was an enlarged D.VII. The bulbous axle fairing housed a fuel tank.

Below: Rumpler Rubild Mb 8231 in French hands; the German insignia have been painted over by French insignia.

The Hannover C.I was the Rumpler C.Ia(Han) and should be included with that type. The Hannover C.II should be included in the Hannover CL.II listing. The Hannover CL.II and Halberstadt CL.II were both originally identified by the designation C.II, although the designations were changed to CL.II when the CL-category was created.

The Pfalz C.I and C.IV were the Rumpler C.IV(Pfal) that Pfalz built under license. The 35 Roland C.I entered in June 1916 were actually the Albatros C.I(Rol) built under license. The 21 Roland C.I shown in February 1917 were actually Roland C.II(Li), the Roland C.II built under license by Linke-Hofmann, but were erroneously reported as "Rol Li C.I" by *Armee Flugpark* 6 during the Battle of Arras in April–May 1917.

The AEG C.IV in October 1915, the Albatros C.IV and C.VII in April 1916, and the Albatros C.X in October 1916 look too early to be correct and are likely transcription errors.

Finally, there are no entries for the DFW C.I, DFW C.II, and DFW C.IV, all of which were used by combat units, albeit in small numbers and for short periods.

Lichtbildflugzeuge

For longer-range, high-altitude reconnaissance the superb Rumpler C.IV was created by installing the powerful 260 hp Mercedes D.IVa into the late-production Rumpler C.III airframe. The C.IV and its many derivatives became the best German high-altitude reconnaissance aircraft. Later models of the Rumpler mounted a variety of over-compressed engines designed to provide more power at high altitude, and these aircraft kept the Rumpler series at the forefront of high-altitude photo-reconnaissance for the rest of the war. Initially categorized as C-types, some of these specialized aircraft were

later designated *Lichtbildflugzeug* (photo aircraft) in acknowledgement of their primary role. Regardless of designation, if the pilot maintained maximum altitude the Rumplers were almost impossible to intercept during their missions.

Lichtbildflugzeug (photographic aircraft) were specialized high-altitude aircraft used for long-range photo-reconnaissance. The only operational types were the Rumpler Rubild and Rubild Mb. Both were based on the Rumpler C.IV airframe equipped with a Messter strip camera and greater fuel capacity. The Rubild, powered by the 260 hp Mercedes D.IVa, was originally designated the Rumpler C.VI. The Rubild Mb was the same aircraft except with the 245 hp Maybach Mb.IVa engine.

CL-Types

Another new role was that of two-seat fighter, first to escort standard C-types on their routine artillery-spotting and reconnaissance tasks, and later for ground-attack using new tactics. These roles placed a premium on good maneuverability, and the CL class was developed for them. The "L" stood for '*licht*', or light C-type, and the new CL designs were smaller than standard two-seaters. The Halberstadt and Hannover companies were the most successful CL designs. Both manufacturers built

Above: For maximum impact in critical situations, a *Schlachtstaffel* of six CL types would operate together at very low altitude. Here a *Schlachtstaffel* of six Halberstadt CL.II ground-attack aircraft speed toward Allied lines for a mass attack.

Above: Looking like a larger, two-bay Halberstadt CL.IV, the Halberstadt C.V was the best general-purpose German two-seater in the last months of the war. It was powered by the 240 hp Benz Bz.IVau over-compressed engine.

Frontbeststand Inventory of *Lichtbildflugzeuge* (Photo-Reconnaissance Planes) at the Front

Manufacturer and Type	1914 31 Aug	31 Oct	31 Dec	1915 28 Feb	30 Apr	30 Jun	31 Aug	31 Oct	31 Dec	1916 28 Feb	30 Apr	30 Jun	31 Aug	31 Oct	31 Dec	1917 28 Feb	30 Apr	30 Jun	31 Aug	31 Oct	31 Dec	1918 28 Feb	30 Apr	30 Jun	31 Aug
Rumpler Rubild																				11	64	51	45	39	99
Rubild Mb																							50	43	78
Total:																				11	64	51	95	82	177

Frontbeststand Inventory of CL-Type Aircraft (Two-Seat Fighters) at the Front

Manufacturer and Type	1914 31 Aug	31 Oct	31 Dec	1915 28 Feb	30 Apr	30 Jun	31 Aug	31 Oct	31 Dec	1916 28 Feb	30 Apr	30 Jun	31 Aug	31 Oct	31 Dec	1917 28 Feb	30 Apr	30 Jun	31 Aug	31 Oct	31 Dec	1918 28 Feb	30 Apr	30 Jun	31 Aug
Halberstadt CL.II																					170	224	342	311	175
CL.IV																									136
Hannover CL.II																					162	295	249	72	31
CL.IIIa																							109	159	233
CL.III																							51	67	29
Total:																					332	519	751	609	604

Right: Operationally important as the best J-type, the Junkers J.I was also historically significant as the world's first production all-metal aircraft. Very rugged, It could return home with 200mm (8") holes in the wings.

Below: The Hannover CL.IIIa was tough and maneuverable, making it an excellent choice for ground-attack or close combat with Allied fighters.

Above: Powered by the same 160 hp Mercedes D.III six-cylinder engine used in the Albatros fighters, the tough, maneuverable Halberstadt CL.II was one of the classic CL types. For its ground-attack mission the gunner is surrounded by hand grenades in rack, signal flares in a belt to the rear of the cockpit, and a flexible machine gun. The pilot had a fixed gun. Other aircraft in the background belong to the same unit, *Schlactstaffel* 27b. Each of the six aircraft in the unit wore the standard factory camouflage plus the unit markings of white chevron, white vertical tail, and black and white fuselage and tailplane stripes. but were differentiated by their tactical number and aircraft name, which was the girlfriend of one of the crewmen of that aircraft. *Brünhilde, tactical #2,* is in the foreground.
Below: *Brünhilde* in color.

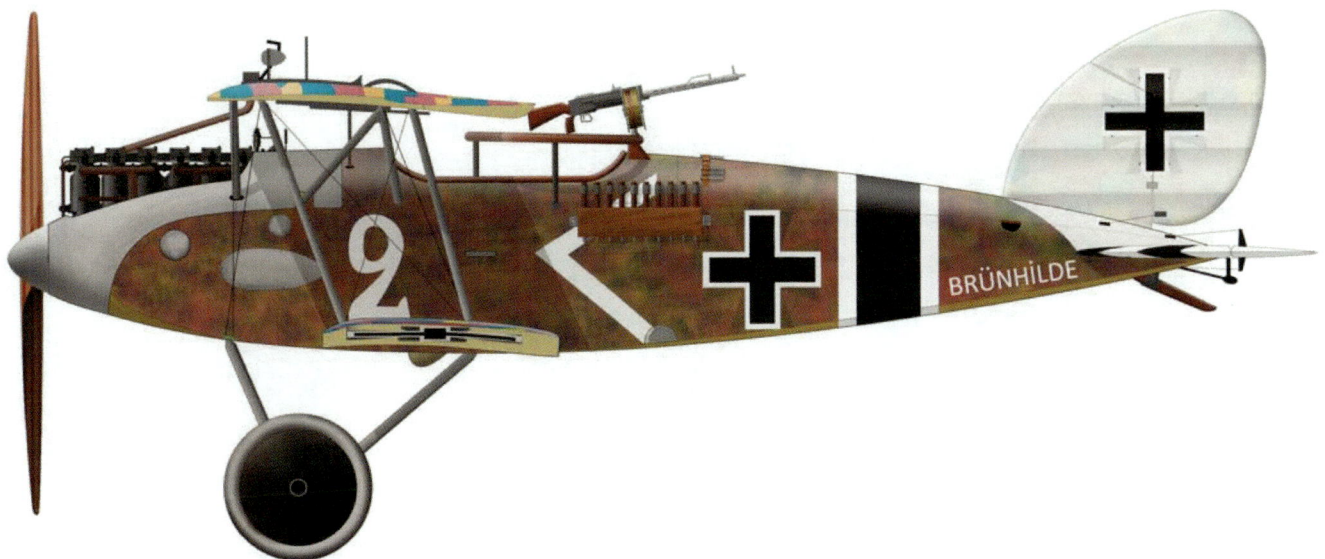

Halberstadt CL.IV tactical number '6' from *Schlasta* 6 flown by *Lt.* Gunther Lüdeke and *Uffz*. Karl Steck, October 1918. *Oblt*. Jurgen Lüdeke commanded *Schlasta* 6 and the death's head unit marking is derived from the Lüdeke brothers' previous service with *Braunschweigesches Husaren-Regiment Nr.*17, *Totenkopf* (Death's Head).

Right: The Junkers CL.I was an all-metal two-seat fighter that arrived too late for combat in WWI because it was much more difficult to manufacture than contemporary airplanes made of wood. It saw extensive postwar service in the German fighting in the Baltic states.

Below: The Halberstadt CL.IV was derived from the CL.II for greater maneuverability by shortening the fuselage and enlarging the horizontal tail; power was the 160 hp Mercedes. This CL.IV is at the USAF Museum.

Above: German fighter units were on the strategic defensive because they were always out-numbered by the Allies. By 1918 the ground-attack units were the offensive arm of the *Luftstreitkräfte*. Here *Schlachtstaffel* 21 is lined up before a mission. Third from right is the commander's aircraft that is shown at the bottom of the previous page. The other aircraft are black with white stripes.

Above: The Hannover CL.II and CL.III were tough, maneuverable two-seat fighters widely used for ground attack. They were distinctive for their biplane tail, which was uncommon on single-engine airplanes. Hannonver continued developed with their CL.V, which was prototyped in both biplane and monoplane tail versions as shown, although production aircraft used the monoplane tail. The Hannover CL.V had a successful postwar career and was built in Norway.

Above: The Halberstadt CLS.I was a smaller development of the CL.IV with 185 hp BMW.IIIa for greater speed and maneuverability, but only prototypes were delivered before the armistice.

fast, maneuverable, robust aircraft that were little larger than contemporary single-seat fighters. Their extra 'sting' in the tail from the gunner made them a difficult opponent for even the best fighters.

The Hannover C.I was re-designated the Aviatik C.I(Han), but before this happened the Hannover C.II appeared, soon to be re-designated to Hannover CL.II when the CL category was established. Confusingly, for a time there were two Hannover C.II types, one the Rumpler C.Ia being built under license, the other the Hannover-designed C.II, later known as the CL.II. The Hannover CL.II retained its designation when the Hannover C.I was re-designated the Aviatik C.I(Han).

Subsequent C-type or CL-type designs received the next consecutive Roman numeral regardless of whether they were C or CL class. For example, Halberstadt two-seat types were the C.I (DFW C.V built under license), CL.II, C.III (prototype C-type), CL.IV, C.V, and the C.VI, C.VII, C.VIII, and C.IX prototypes.

J-Types

Still another role for which specialized aircraft were needed was infantry cooperation. In those days before easily-portable voice radios, there was no good way for headquarters to keep in contact with the moving front line of infantry during an attack. To solve this problem, two-seat aircraft were flown at low level to observe the moving front of the infantry attack and keep headquarters informed of its progress so the attack could be properly supported with reinforcements, re-supply, and adjusting the advance to enemy actions. Standard C-type aircraft were vulnerable to small-arms fire at the low altitudes they had to fly to succeed in this mission and losses started to become unacceptable. The obvious solution was a two-seat airplane armored against small-arms fire, and this new *Idflieg* requirement created the J-Class. The letter 'I' was not used to avoid confusion with the numeral '1',

Above: Powered by the same 160 hp Mercedes D.III six-cylinder engine used in the Albatros fighters, the AEG C.IV was a competent early C-type whose main claim to fame was its welded steel tube construction. Unremarkable though it was, it served as the basis for both the AEG J-types and the AEG N.I night bomber.

so the new class of armored two-seaters was called the 'J' class, 'J' following 'I' in the alphabet. The J-type was introduced to combat in the summer of 1917 and the excellent results the type achieved lead to substantial orders and a steady increase in the numbers at the front despite combat attrition. According to Hoff, a total of 238 J-types were listed in the *Frontbestand* for October 1918.

Three manufacturers designed aircraft to the J-type requirement, and all three were placed in production. Most successful and most technically significant was the Junkers J.I, the first all-metal production airplane in the world. Corrugated metal was used for the skin for sufficient stiffness, and the engine and crewmembers were surrounded by an armored 'tub' that protected them from ground fire. The Junkers J.I became an immediate success and was in production and use until the end of the war. It had two main limitations; first, its innovative metal structure was time-consuming to build, limiting production. Second, it was very heavy, which limited the size of airfields it could use and earned it the nickname 'furniture van' from its crews. The Junkers J.I was known to survive 200mm shell holes in its wings, and none are confirmed to have been shot down by enemy fighters.

Because more J-types were need than Junkers could produce, the AEG company modified their standard C.IV reconnaissance plane, which featured a structure of welded steel tubes, into an armored

Left: The AEG J.I infantry airplane was developed from the C.IV by bolting armor plate around the engine and cockpit and replacing its 160 hp Mercedes D.III with a more powerful 200 hp Benz Bz.IV to carry its extra 400 kg weight. To improve maneuverability ailerons were fitted to all four wings. The pilot's fixed gun was removed because diving at ground targets to strafe them was viewed as unwise in the heavy J.I.

Frontbeststand Inventory of J-Type Aircraft (Armored Infantry Cooperation) at the Front

Manufacturer and Type		1914			1915						1916						1917						1918			
		31 Aug	31 Oct	31 Dec	28 Feb	30 Apr	30 Jun	31 Aug	31 Oct	31 Dec	28 Feb	30 Apr	30 Jun	31 Aug	31 Oct	31 Dec	28 Feb	30 Apr	30 Jun	31 Aug	31 Oct	31 Dec	28 Feb	30 Apr	30 Jun	31 Aug
AEG	J.I																		4	1	11	35	55	66	43	28
	J.II																							15	65	63
	J.																		3							
Albatros	J.I																					37	42	33	51	16
	J.II																									19
Junkers	J.I																			1	1	4	16	25	25	60
Total:																			7	2	12	76	113	139	184	186

Above & Below: A series of running modifications were made during J.I production to improve survivability and maneuverability. These included doubling the lift-bracing wires and control cables to reduce vulnerability to ground fire. The fuselage was lengthened to improve stability, and wing area was enlarged by extending the chord, improving lift. Two downward-firing machine guns were fitted in addition to the observer's flexible guns; the muzzles can be seen in the photo above protruding below the fuselage. The AEG J.II was developed from the J.I through a series of changes, and these photos show the final J.II production configuration with horn balances on all control surfaces. The horn balances reduced control pressures and enabled the pilot to maneuver the heavy airplane more quickly. Although not as resistant to ground fire as the all-metal Junkers J.I, the AEG J-types were good aircraft that were much easier to build and became the most numerous J-types at the Front.

Above & Below: The powerful Albatros company, the largest German airplane manufacturer, produced the Albatros J.I (above) from the earlier Albatros C.X and C.XII types by adding armor to the cockpit and replacing the 260 hp Mercedes D.IVa with the 200 hp Benz Bz.IV. The reduced power and heavy weight greatly reduced performance and flying qualities, but the airplanes depended on their armor for protection. Later two downward-firing machine guns were fitted in addition to the observer's flexible guns. Unsurprisingly, the crews complained about the vulnerability of the J.I's unarmored engine, and the J.II (shown below), with fully-armored engine, replaced the J.I in production. The boxy lines of the J.II's engine cowling are the result of the armor plate. The J.II also had enlarged horn balances on its ailerons to reduce control pressures for enhanced maneuverability. The wooden structure of the Albatros J-types was the most vulnerable to ground fire of all the J-types, and accordingly they were built in the smallest numbers despite being easy to build.

J-type by attaching armor plate to the sides and under-surfaces of the engine and cockpit. Not integrating the armor into the primary structure was not as elegant a solution as the Junkers design, but resulted in an airplane, the AEG J.I, that was much easier and faster to build. Although not as

impervious to ground fire as its Junkers sibling, the AEG was a good airplane for its role.

As the fighting continued the cooperation duties of the J-types evolved into more aggressive ground-attack, blurring the distinction between the role of the J-types and CL-types. Experience led to the

```
Leergewicht: 1400 kg
Nutzlast:       410
Gesammtgew:1810 kg
```

Above & Below: By 1918 Allied tanks became a major problem for the German Army, and anti-tank weapons became more important. The 20mm Becker cannon was accordingly fitted to a number of Albatros J.Is on a simple mount on the side of the gunner's cockpit as shown here.

Above: The 20mm Becker cannon fitted to the Albatros J.Is proved to be effective anti-tank weapons, and 20 Albatros J.II aircraft were fitted with the 20mm Becker in an improved mount in the floor of the gunner's cockpit shown here; the front of the aircraft is at the top of the photo. Extra magazines for the Becker are stacked on the sides of the armored cockpit and extra drums of machine gun ammunition are stored at the rear. Twenty AEG J.II aircraft were delivered with a similar Becker installation.

addition of more armament to the AEG J.I in the form of a downward-firing pair of machine guns mounted in the observer's cockpit and fired by him. The guns were normally angled to fire 45° below horizontal and aimed by the gunner observing the ground through a small hole in the floor in the front corner of his cockpit. The additional weight of this gun installation was too much for the heavy Junkers, which never received additional armament and made do with only the observer's flexible gun.

Continued development by AEG resulted in the AEG J.II, which had revised controls for better maneuverability, doubled bracing wires and inboard wing spars for reduced vulnerability to ground fire, and downward-firing machine guns fitted as standard.

To destroy Allied tanks, which were becoming a serious problem for the infantry, in September 1918 20 AEG J.IIs were delivered with a downward-firing 20mm Becker cannon on a flexible mount for the gunner. The AEG J. listed in June 1917 must have been the J.I since the J.II did not appear until 1918.

Albatros was the third manufacturer to produce a J-type. The Albatros J.I inherited its wooden structure from the C.XII reconnaissance two-seater from which it was developed. Unlike all the other J-types, the Albatros J.I had armor around

An compentent but unremarkable airplane, the AEG C.IV nevertheless was the ancestor of the AEG N.I and the AEG J.I and J.II. All AEG aircraft were of welded steel tube construction covered by fabric. This C.IV is in standard factory sprayed camouflage finish with the black unit marking of *Schutzstaffel* 6 in 1916.

This early production J.II looks like a late J.I; it does not yet have the horn-balanced control surfaces of the final J.II configuration which made the J.II more maneuverable. The two machine guns in the observer's cockpit fixed to fire downward at 45° are clearly visible. The observer also had a flexible machine gun to defend against fighters and strafe ground targets.

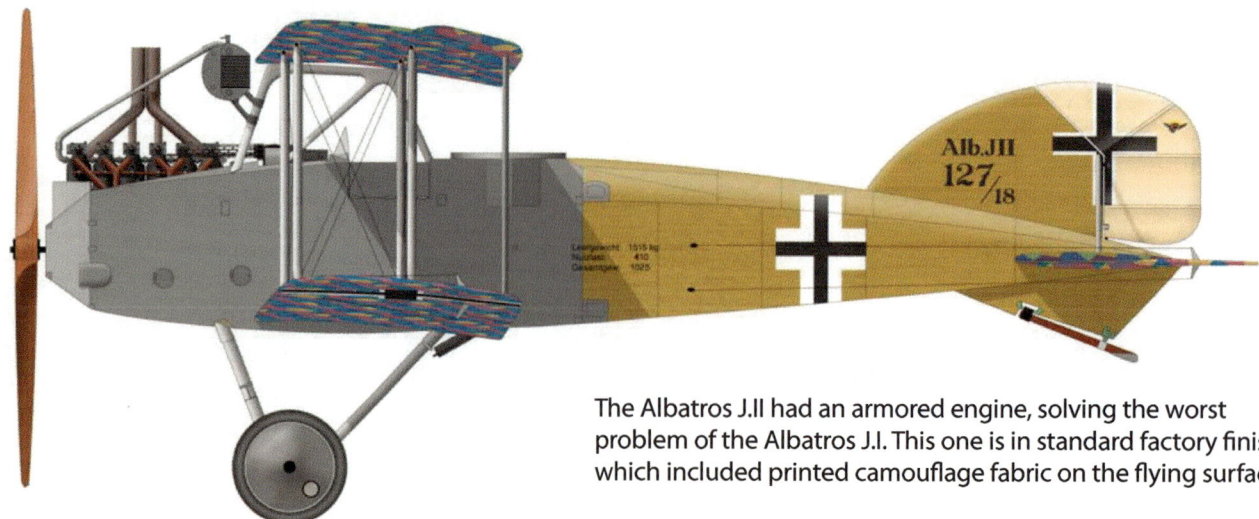

The Albatros J.II had an armored engine, solving the worst problem of the Albatros J.I. This one is in standard factory finish, which included printed camouflage fabric on the flying surfaces.

Despite being the heaviest J-type, the Junkers J.I was the fastest due to its more aerodynamic design, partly due to its lack of drag-producing bracing wires.

the cockpit but, to save weight, it had no armor protecting the engine. Like the AEG J.II, 20 Albatros J.Is were fitted with a 20mm Becker cannon on a flexible mount for the gunner for destroying tanks. Others had the pair of downward-firing machine guns as installed on the AEG J.I.

Complaints from crewmen about the vulnerability of the Albatros J.I's engine to ground fire resulted in a revised design, the J.II, with fully-armored engine, that succeeded the Albatros J.I in production.

The AEG J-types were the most valuable; they could be built in much greater quantity than the superior Junkers and were much less vulnerable to ground fire than the wooden Albatros J-types.

S-Types

The increasing important of anti-tank weapons lead to *Idflieg* creating the S-type. The S-type was basically an evolved J-type whose primary purpose was ground attack, especially destroying tanks. The requirement was for a two-seat armored biplane with 20mm Becker cannon fitted for anti-tank duties. The gunner also had a flexible machine gun to defend the aircraft against enemy fighters. The Ago S.I, the only S-type apparently completed before the armistice, was too late to go into production or operation.

Above & Right: The massive Ago S.I was the only S-type completed before the armistice. The drawing at right shows the armor plate and the mounting of the 20mm Becker cannon for anti-tank duties. The gunner also had a flexible machine gun to defend against enemy fighters.

Frontbeststand Inventory of N-Type Aircraft (Single-Engine Night Bombers) at the Front

Manufacturer and Type	1914			1915						1916						1917						1918			
	31 Aug	31 Oct	31 Dec	28 Feb	30 Apr	30 Jun	31 Aug	31 Oct	31 Dec	28 Feb	30 Apr	30 Jun	31 Aug	31 Oct	31 Dec	28 Feb	30 Apr	30 Jun	31 Aug	31 Oct	31 Dec	28 Feb	30 Apr	30 Jun	31 Aug
AEG N.I																				2	31	37	19	7	4
Sablatnig N.I																								2	9
Total:																				2	31	37	19	9	13

Above: The versatile AEG C.IV was developed into the AEG N.I night bomber by enlarging its wingspan and fitting three bays of struts. The bracing trusses fitted to both upper wing spars to strengthen the wing to withstand the increased bending forces are clearly visible, as is the typical AEG night-bomber camouflage.

Left: The Sablatnig N.I was the only other operational N-type; only 45 were built.

N-Types

Standard C-types were used throughout the war for light bombing both during the day and at night. However, resource-starved Germany wanted aircraft that could carry a heavier bombload at night while using a less powerful engine that used less fuel. The desire for a single-engine night bomber of greater bombload than standard C-types led to new designs and yet another category of two-seat warplane, the N-type, or *Nachtflugzeug* (night aircraft).

At least five manufacturers submitted designs to this requirement, but only two reached production and operational service. First and most numerous was AEG. The AEG N.I was yet another design derived from its standard C.IV reconnaissance plane. The wingspan was extended for greater lifting capacity for the heavier bombload desired, and the C.IV's 160 hp Mercedes D.III engine, which was in great demand for fighter production, was replaced with the less popular 150 hp Benz Bz.III. The longer-span wing failed repeated load tests due to bending; this was solved effectively if inelegantly by strengthening both upper wing spars by addition of external bracing trusses. Approximately 200 AEG N.I aircraft were built and served anonymously with standard two-seater units.

The Sablatnig company also designed an N-type, the Sablatnig N.I, that was produced in small numbers and these also served at the front. Neither N-type was built in large numbers because Germany had excellent twin-engine night bombers that were preferred by their crews and carried more bombs.

Fighters

Monoplane Fighters (E Types)

In the spring of 1915 French pilot Roland Garros armed his aircraft with a machine gun fixed to fire forward with deflector plates on the propeller blades to protect them. He shot down three German aircraft before he came down behind German lines due to mechanical problems. After capture his crude bullet deflector was given to Anthony Fokker to copy. Fokker quickly responded with a synchronizing gear to enable a machine gun to fire through the propeller arc without striking the propeller, and the airborne arms race was on in earnest.

Fokker mounted the synchronized gun on one of his single-seat monoplanes. Monoplane is *Eindecker* in German, and *Idflieg* designated the resulting production fighter the Fokker E.I, with E-type being the new designation for armed monoplane. From his E.I Fokker developed new fighters using more powerful rotary engines up through the E.IV.

Before the war the Pfalz company had licensed the rights to produce French Morane-Saulnier designs in Germany. After the Fokker E-types appeared, Pfalz developed a series of similar fighters derived

Above: Oswald Boelcke in Fokker E.I serial E.13/15, an aircraft also flown by Max Immelmann. With its single synchronized machine gun the Fokker E.I was the world's first purpose-built fighter aircraft design, and both Boelcke and Immelmann started their careers as fighter pilots in the type and became famous aces. The E.I was powered by a 7-cylinder, 80 hp Oberursel U.0 engine.

Right: Oswald Boelcke stands in front of a Fokker E.II or E.III, as shown by its 9-cylinder, 100 hp Oberursel U.I engine. The E.II used the same airframe as the E.I; the only difference between the two types was the engine. The E.III had the same engine as the E.II but a slightly longer wingspan. These minor differences are not very noticeable in most photographs, frequently making it difficult to distinguish between these early fighter types. All were armed with a single synchronized machine gun.

Above: Max Immelmann's ground crew with his Fokker E.IV serial E.127/15. The E.IV had a two-row, 160 hp Oberursel U.III rotary engine, and its larger cowling with additional cooling holes is clearly seen here. The additional power made the E.IV noticeably faster than the earlier Fokker fighters and enabled it to carry two machine guns. This makes the E.IV easy to distinguish from the earlier types, all of which look much alike and are often difficult to distinguish in photos.

Below: The Fokker E.II in the left foreground is shown with Pfalz E.I serial 215/15 in the middle and a Pfalz E.II in the background. Although of similar configuration, the Pfalz fighters, derived from the pre-war Morane-Saulnier H, exhibit some noticeable differences, including the shape of the rudder, the iron cross insignia on their elevators, and their color scheme of unpainted linen with black edging on the wings and fuselage. All these differences went unnoticed by Allied aircrew in the heat of combat!

Frontbeststand Inventory of E-Type Aircraft (Monoplane Fighters) at the Front

Manufacturer and Type	1914 31 Aug	1914 31 Oct	1914 31 Dec	1915 28 Feb	1915 30 Apr	1915 30 Jun	1915 31 Aug	1915 31 Oct	1915 31 Dec	1916 28 Feb	1916 30 Apr	1916 30 Jun	1916 31 Aug	1916 31 Oct	1916 31 Dec	1917 28 Feb	1917 30 Apr	1917 30 Jun	1917 31 Aug	1917 31 Oct	1917 31 Dec	1918 28 Feb	1918 30 Apr	1918 30 Jun	1918 31 Aug
Fokker E.I						4	17	23	26	12	22	3	1												
E.II							2	8	14	20	13	4	5	2	1					2					
E.III							3	23	40	67	110	101	64	28	11	2	1	1		8	7				
E.IV								1	6	6	28	29	25	16	2										
E.V (D.VIII)																									80
Pfalz E.I								2	14	26	27	13	11	3	1										
E.II									6	11	20	30	17	3											
E.III								1	1		4	8													
E.IV											5		1												
E.V												3													
SSW E.I														5	2	1	1								
Unknown			2																						
Total:			2			4	22	58	107	142	229	191	124	57	17	3	2	1		10	7				80

from their license-built Morane-Saulnier H aircraft. Development of the Pfalz monoplane fighters paralleled Fokker development with the addition of the Pfalz E.V powered by a six-cylinder water-cooled engine. No Fokker E-type used a similar engine.

The appearance of the British D.H.2 pusher biplane and, more importantly, the French Nieuport 11 sesquiplane at the front ended the technical superiority of the Fokker (and Pfalz) monoplanes, which essentially disappeared from the front by the end of 1916 in favor of new biplane fighters. Several Fokker E.II and E.III appeared later in 1917, a direct result of the introduction of the Fokker Dr.I rotary-powered triplane fighter. In this case, the E.II and E.III aircraft were to give the pilots some experience with rotary engines before they transitioned to the Fokker Dr.I.

In August 1918 the new Fokker E.V parasol monoplane briefly revived the E-type designation. However, after inflight wing failures due to shoddy

Below: Like the Fokker E.IV, the Pfalz E.IV featured twin guns and the two-row, 160 hp Oberursel U.III engine. The E.IV had larger wings than the E.II to handle the additional weight and a longer tail to balance the heavier engine and two guns.

Fok. E III 315/16

Above: Fokker E.III flown by *Oblt*. Hans Berr, August 1916. The E-types were becoming obsolete by this time and German pilots desperately needed the new biplane fighters just starting to arrive. Berr scored 10 victories and was awarded the *Pour le Mérite*, but was killed in action 6 April 1917.

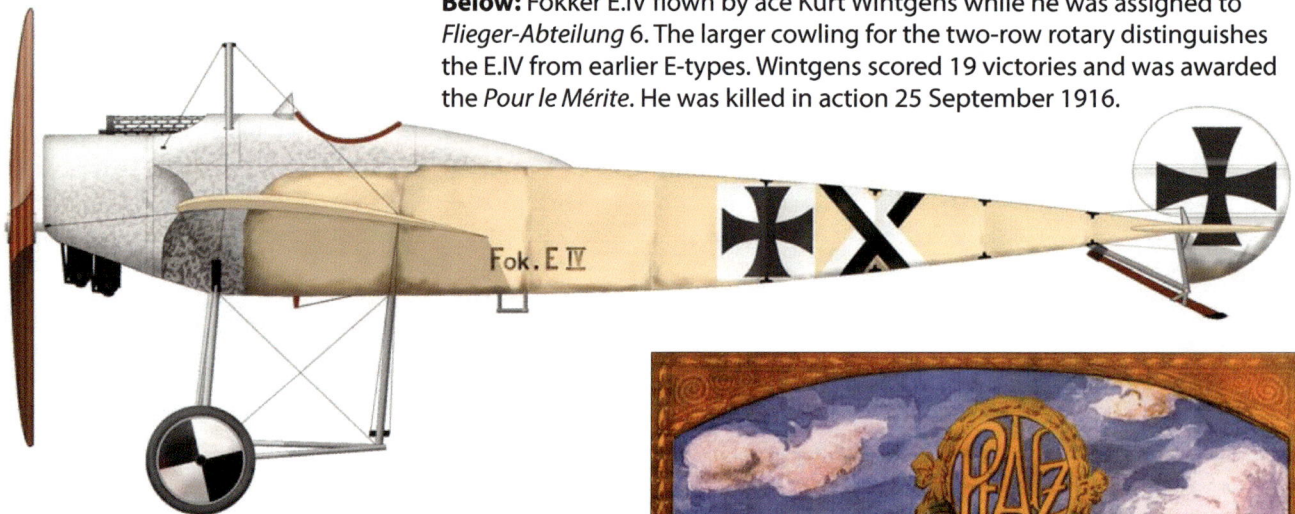

Below: Fokker E.IV flown by ace Kurt Wintgens while he was assigned to *Flieger-Abteilung* 6. The larger cowling for the two-row rotary distinguishes the E.IV from earlier E-types. Wintgens scored 19 victories and was awarded the *Pour le Mérite*. He was killed in action 25 September 1916.

Fok. E IV

Right: Pfalz company poster.
Below: Pfalz company decal.

PFALZ - FLUGZEUGE

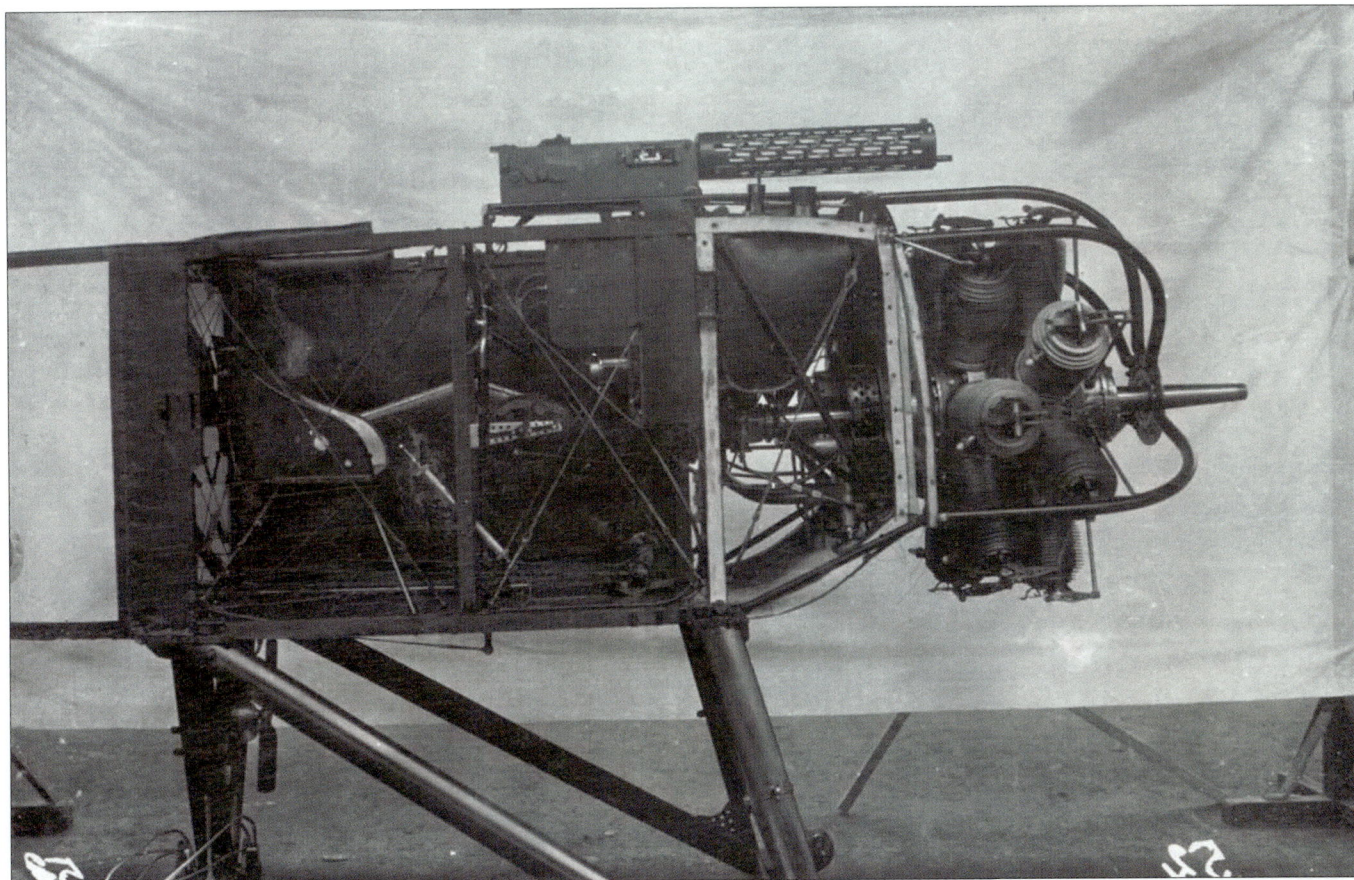

Above: This candid view shows the structure of the Pfalz E.IV with its two-row, 160 hp Oberursel U.III.

Right: One Pfalz E.II served with FA 300 "Pascha" in Palestine. Pilot *Lt.* Hans Henkel poses with his ground crew.

Below: The Pfalz E.V was the only Pfalz E-type with a water-cooled engine, a 100 hp Mercedes D.I. It was faster than the more powerful E.IV but mounted only one gun. Superior biplane fighters were already arriving at the front and only 20 were built. The pre-war design used by Pfalz was not stressed for combat maneuvers and after some structural failures, all Pfalz E-types were withdrawn from the front.

Above: A few SSW E.I fighters reached the front. These two are shown during construction in the factory, but by the time these reached the Front the *Eindecker* era was drawing to a close as higher-performance biplane fighters were appearing.

workmanship, the aircraft soon had to be sent back to the factory for new wings. When they reappeared in October, their designation had been changed to Fokker D.VIII; in the interim *Idflieg* decided to use the D-type designation for all single-seat fighters regardless of configuration.

The E-class did not exist in 1914, so the two unknown types listed for December 1914 are clearly a transcription error.

Biplane Fighters (D Types)

The appearance of superior Allied biplane fighters at the front made *Idflieg* realize that the era of the Fokker monoplanes was drawing to a close and new fighters of biplane configuration were required. Thus the D-type, or single-seat biplane fighter, was born. The robust, maneuverable Halberstadt fighters arrived at the front first, followed shortly by the breakthrough Albatros fighters. Powered by the new 160 hp Mercedes D.III engine, the Albatros fighters were streamlined, fast, maneuverable, and first to be armed with two machine guns, a feature that set the standard for the rest of the war. The powerful Albatros fighters immediately achieved technical superiority over Allied fighters, and as more arrived

at the *Jastas* they achieved air superiority that lasted until the advent of new Allied designs in April–June 1917.

The same excellent Mercedes engine was available to other German manufacturers, but none of their designs matched the Albatros. The early Fokker D-types were clearly inferior to the Albatros in all performance respects, and the Roland D.I–D.III, while fast and robust, lacked maneuverability and had a generally poor forward view for the pilot.

From summer 1917 onward was a trying time for German fighter pilots because German fighter design stagnated. A major problem was stagnation of German aero-engine design. Once the excellent 160 hp Mercedes D.III was established in mass production, followed by the dramatic impact of the Albatros fighters, *Idflieg* was content to mass-produce the Albatros fighters and the Mercedes engine that powered them.

Fearing disruption of engine production by introduction of a new type, *Idflieg* failed to push engine development, with the result that the next generation of fighter designs had to use existing engines. This was a serious mistake; the engine is the heart of an aircraft and determines the

Above & Right: The Halberstadt D.II powered by the 120 hp Mercedes D.II was the first German biplane fighter to reach the front. Despite its delicate appearance, with no fixed fin, it was a very robust aircraft. Fitted with a single machine gun, it out-performed and out-maneuvered the preceding German *Eindeckers* in every respect and was at least as good as the DH.2 and Nieuport 11 fighters the Allies were using when it appeared. Some aircraft were modified at the unit level to carry two synchronized machine guns. The later Halberstadt CL.II bears a strong family resemblance. Above *Lt*. Kirmaier poses by his Halberstadt serving with *Jasta* 4.

limits of its performance. However, instead of developing new engines, which takes extensive time and resources that were limited in wartime Germany, *Idflieg* instead focused on advanced structures and aerodynamics to achieve better performance. In contrast, the resource-rich Allies pursued engine development to increase power for better performance and relied on existing structural methods and materials to facilitate mass production.

A good example of the difference in the two approaches is the contrast between the last fighters introduced into combat before the armistice. Germany introduced the Fokker D.VIII, a parasol monoplane that was the minimum possible fighter.

It had an innovative, cantilever wooden wing and welded steel tube fuselage and tail covered by fabric. These materials were fairly available even in Germany, especially the plywood for the wing. Introduced in August 1918, it was powered by the same rotary engine used in the Fokker E.III in the summer of 1915! The D.VIII thus combined a 1915 engine with 1918 structural and aerodynamic designs. In contrast the Sopwith Snipe, a larger, more powerful derivative of the 1916 Camel, was powered by a new rotary engine. The Snipe combined a 1918 engine with 1916 structural design and aerodynamics. Interestingly, the designs were competitive in performance.

In mid-1917 the German dilemma was that

Above: Soon after the Halberstadt D.II reached the front the Albatros D.I also started reaching German units. Using the more powerful 160 hp Mercedes D.III engine, the Albatros carried two guns and was faster than the Halberstadt although not as maneuverable. The Albatros fighters quickly established technical superiority over Allied aircraft in the autumn of 1916 and fought until the end of the war. The D.I's side-mounted radiators seem incongruous on its streamlined fuselage.

Above: The Albatros D.II prototype at Johannisthal. Serial 386/16, it was allocated to Oswald Boelcke; this was the airplane he was flying when he experienced his fatal mid-air collision with a squadron mate. Pilots liked the D.I but said the upper wing was too high above their sightline and blocked too much of the view from the cockpit, so the wing was lowered to just above the pilots' sightline in the D.II, requiring a different cabane design. Otherwise the two types were identical. Late production D.IIs replaced the ear radiators with lower-drag airfoil radiators in the upper wing center section.

Frontbeststand Inventory of D-Type Aircraft (Biplane Fighters) at the Front

Manufacturer and Type		1914			1915						1916						1917						1918			
		31 Aug	31 Oct	31 Dec	28 Feb	30 Apr	30 Jun	31 Aug	31 Oct	31 Dec	28 Feb	30 Apr	30 Jun	31 Aug	31 Oct	31 Dec	28 Feb	30 Apr	30 Jun	31 Aug	31 Oct	31 Dec	28 Feb	30 Apr	30 Jun	31 Aug
AEG	D.I																			1						
Albatros	D.I													1	50	39	28	20	17	12	9	8	5	6	1	3
	D.II													1	28	214	150	107	72	44	11	6	2	2	2	2
	D.III															13	137	327	303	385	446	423	357	174	82	52
	D.V																		216	424	526	513	250	131	91	20
	D.Va																				53	186	475	928	604	307
	D Lf																	2								
Aviatik	D.I																	15								
	D.III																	4								
DFW	D.II																		1							
Euler	D.II														2							11	16	13	6	1
Fokker	D.I													10	74	4	5	5	6	2	1					
	D.II													10	49	68	49	33	26	10			6			
	D.III													7	6	34	7		1		4			11	11	10
	D.IV													2		2					4					
	D.V																3	6	4	4	4	12	25	19	6	3
	D.VI																								21	27
	D.VII																							19	407	828
Halberstadt	D.I													6			12	16	14	1	2					
	D.II												6	5		55	5	2	14	16	3	2	1		1	1
	D.III										1		2	20	32	17	12	9	8	6	7	5	1	2	2	2
	D.V													17	32		39	11	6	9	5	3	2			
LVG	D.I																61	47	18							
	D.II																1									
Pfalz	D.III																		3	145	276		182	13	13	3
	D.IIIa																					114	261	433	289	166
	D.VIII																								14	19
	D.XII																								5	168
Roland	D.I														1	7	12	2	1							
	D.II																22	97	41	10	2					
	D.IIa																		128	102	6	3				
	D.III																						9	14		
	D.VIa																								38	58
	D.VIb																								17	12
SSW	D.I																	2								
	D.III																							4	4	6
	D.IV																									3
Total:											1		8	62	265	485	562	686	875	1030	1224	1566	1592	1769	1614	1691

Right: Developed from the earlier Roland C.II two-seater, the Roland D.I fighter had two guns and a 160 hp Mercedes D.III engine. It was fast but the pilots' forward view was poor, and the design was quickly revised as the Roland D.II to remedy that limitation, particularly problematic for a fighter.

the Albatros D.V was no real improvement over its predecessors; in fact, lightening its structure weakened it, leading to failures of the lower wing spar. The wing was strong enough statically; the failure mechanism was flutter due to the lower wing spar being too far aft in the airfoil and insufficiently stiff in torsion. Flutter was not understood at the time and various modifications reduced the problem but did not solve it.

A number of competing prototypes using the same engine and armament and similar technology failed to reach production. The Pfalz D.III was the only design that did reach production, but other than being structurally sounder than the Albatros due to is two-spar lower wing, it unsurprisingly offered no noticeable performance improvement.

The Albatros D Lf in the *Frontbestand* was likely a naval *Landflugzeug* (LF = landplane) whose pilot was flying with an Army *Jasta* to gain combat experience. At the time of the entry that most likely would have been an Albatros D.III.

The Aviatik D.I and D.III listed in February 1917 were the Halberstadt D.II(Av) built under license by Aviatik. The DFW D.II listed in June 1917 may be one of the DFW *Floh* (flea) prototypes then under development that may have been sent to the front for evaluation.

The Euler D.II entry for October 1916 must be an error; it was type-tested on 8 January 1917 prior to an order for 30 production fighters placed in March 1917. The unarmed Euler D.II served as a transition trainer to familiarize pilots with rotary engine aircraft. Similarly, the build-up of Fokker D.V rotary-powered fighters in late 1917 and early 1918 was due to moving these fighters near the front for training pilots transitioning to the rotary-powered Fokker Dr.I.

The LVG D.I was the Albatros D.II(LVG) built under license and should have been included in the Albatros D.II entries. The LVG D.II was the LVG D 12 biplane fighter prototype developed in late 1916 and, if this entry is not an error, sent to the front for evaluation.

According to Hoff, a total of 2,454 D-types were listed in the *Frontbestand* for October 1918. However, this seems unlikely since the Germans had great trouble fulfilling the armistice terms of delivering 2,000 aircraft of all types to the Allies.

Below: Six-victory ace Emil Meinecke and his Halberstadt D.V in Turkey after a hard combat with British aircraft.

Halberstadt D.II serving with *Jasta* 5. Factory camouflage is used with a black rudder and tactical number '7'. The pilot is unknown.

Halberstadt D.V in the winter of 1916/1917. Factory camouflage is used with tactical number '2'. The pilot is unknown.

The lighter, more streamlined Albatros D.V was the next Albatros fighter to reach the front in May 1917. This captured D.Va is on display in Australia. Germany had to wait for the Fokker D.VII to regain technical superiority in fighters.

Above: The Albatros D.III was based on the late-production D.II airframe with a new wing cellule inspired by the Nieuport sesquiplanes. Reports of the Nieuports' maneuverability and performance inspired *Idflieg* to send captured Nieuports around to different German manufacturers for inspection. Albatros based the wings of their D.III on the Nieuport design, producing the famous "V-Strutter" Albatros fighters. The new wings provided better performance and downward vision than the previous wing, but inherited the weakness of the Nieuport's single-spar lower wing. Unknown to *Idflieg*, Nieuports had already experienced failures of their lower wing, and the faster, heavier Albatros D.III suffered even more. The problem became acute when the Albatros D.V, a lightened D.III design, reached combat in May 1917.

Above: The Albatros D.V used the wings from the D.III together with a lightened, more streamlined fuselage. The attractive headrest soon disappeared from production as pilots complained it impaired their view to the rear. Committed to mass production before the full implications of the lower wing spar weakness were known, the D.V performed no better than the D.III and was not as robust. Lower wing failures now became a major problem that dogged the D.V and subsequent D.Va despite numerous attemps at a solution. The wing was strong enough statically, frustrating attempts to understand and solve the problem. The root of the problem, not understood at the time, was that the single spar in the lower wing was too far aft. The spar was located at 40% of the chord behind the leading edge, but the center of lift on a wing is at 25% chord. That meant lift on the wing constantly tried to twist the wing around its spar. At higher speeds and during high-G maneuvering the greater lift caused more twisting, leading to flutter (the wing oscillating around the spar) and structural failure of the spar. This was frequently fatal and the danger of it certainly limited the maneuvers a pilot could make during combat, which was a major liability made even worse by the superior performance of the new generation of Allied fighters introduced as the D.V arrived at the front. A meter stick has been set on this plane for scale.

This Albatros D.I flown by *Lt.* Dieter Collin wears the standard factory finish other than the individual marking of the letters "Co" for Collin's last name. An ace with 13 victories, he was killed in action 13 August 1917 while *Staffelfuhrer* of Jasta 56. Later the factory used darker stain to finish the wood fuselage as shown below.

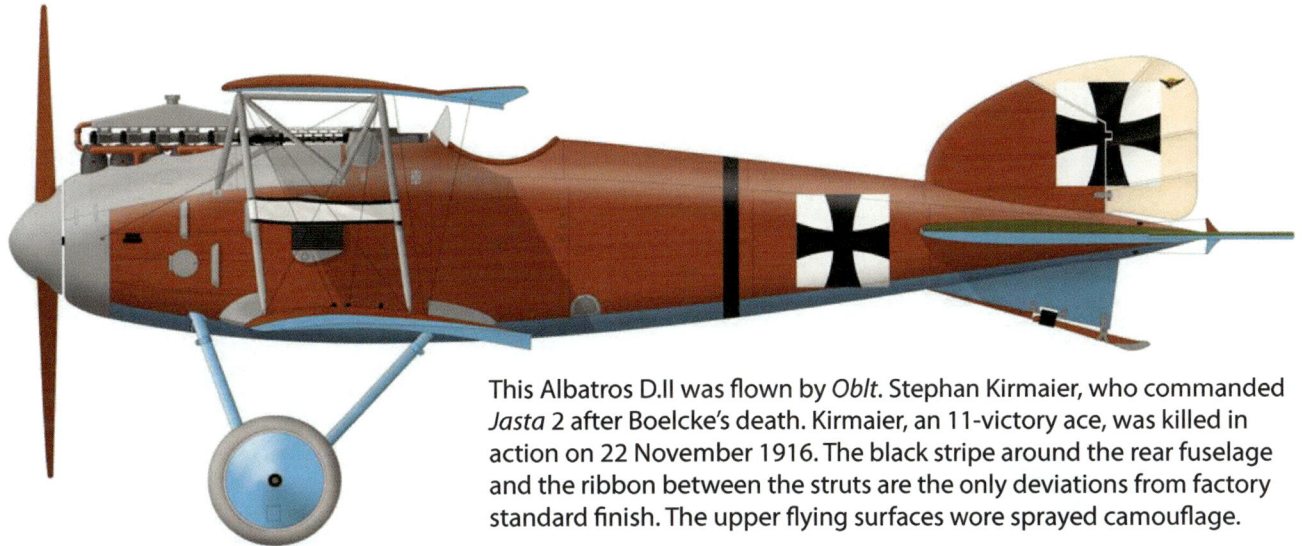

This Albatros D.II was flown by *Oblt.* Stephan Kirmaier, who commanded *Jasta* 2 after Boelcke's death. Kirmaier, an 11-victory ace, was killed in action on 22 November 1916. The black stripe around the rear fuselage and the ribbon between the struts are the only deviations from factory standard finish. The upper flying surfaces wore sprayed camouflage.

Albatros D.III flown by *Lt.* Hermann Frommherz of *Jasta* Boelcke. It was painted an overall light blue at the *Jasta*. The black and white markings were also added there. Frommherz became an ace with 32 victories and was nominated for the *Pour le Mérite*, but the Kaiser abdicated before signing the award and Frommherz never officially received it.

This Roland D.II(Pfal) flew with *Kest* 4. Using the same engine and guns as the Albatros fighters, the Roland fighters were strong and fast but had mediocre maneuverability and handling characteristics, and the pilot's forward field of view was poor. As a result the Rolands served in relatively small numbers while the Albatros was built in great quantity.

Fokker D.II 540/16 flown by *Lt.d.R.* Otto Kissenberth at *KEK* Ensisheim, 12 October 1916. On that day Kissenberth intercepted a combined British and French bombing raid on the German city of Oberndorf, and scored his first three victories in this machine. It has a three-color camouflage scheme that was applied, or modified, at *KEK* Ensisheim. Kissenberth went on to score 20 victories and was awarded the *Pour le Mérite*.

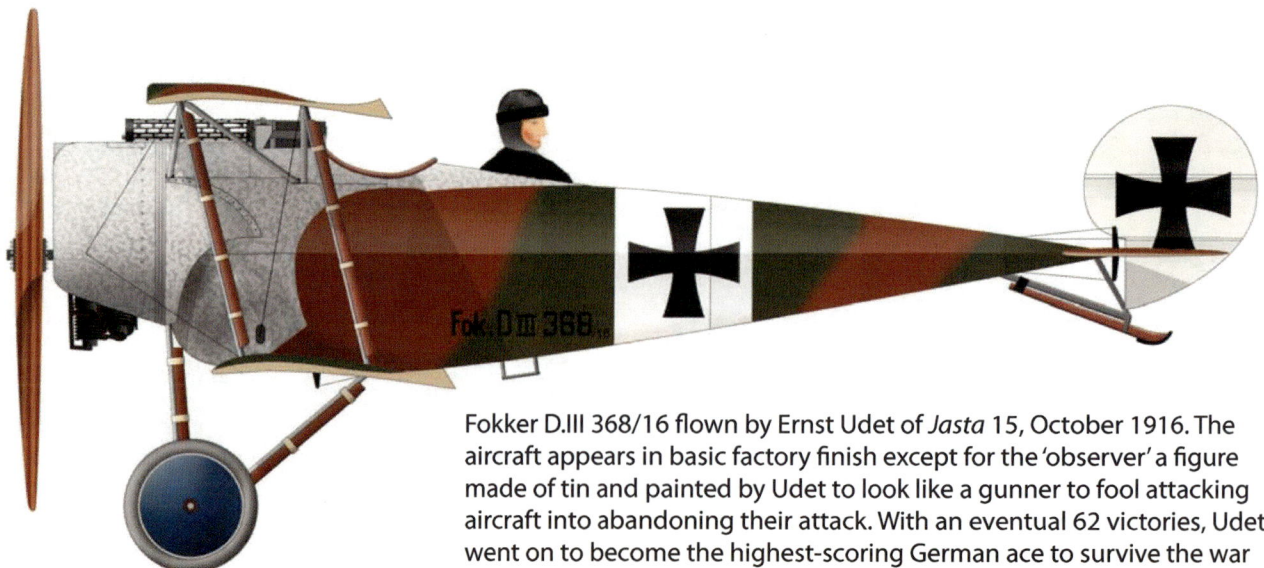

Fokker D.III 368/16 flown by Ernst Udet of *Jasta* 15, October 1916. The aircraft appears in basic factory finish except for the 'observer' a figure made of tin and painted by Udet to look like a gunner to fool attacking aircraft into abandoning their attack. With an eventual 62 victories, Udet went on to become the highest-scoring German ace to survive the war and second only to the Red Baron. He was awarded the *Pour le Mérite*.

Above: The speedy Roland D.II was developed from the Roland D.I to improve the forward view for the pilot. Powered by the same 160 hp Mercedes engine as the Albatros fighters and mounting the same armament of two guns, the Roland D.II was a strong, fast airplane. Unfortunately, the D.II still had inadequate visibility directly forward, a serious problem in a fighter, and lacked the good maneuverability and handling qualities of the Albatros. It was not the solution *Idflieg* was looking for, and production and operational use were limited compared to the Albatros. Many Rolands were sent to the Eastern Front, where they could be useful in the more permissive combat environment there.

Below: Roland developed the D.III from their D.II in another attempt to improve the pilots field of view forward, and clearly succeeded. Unfortunately, maneuverability, handling, and performance were essentially the same as the D.II. The lower wing chord was reduced on the D.III for better downward view as indicated by the converging interplane struts.

Fokker Failures

The eclipse of the *Eindeckers* by better biplane fighters was a problem for Fokker. Fokker designed a number of biplane fighters that, obviously descended from his monoplanes, were not only mediocre performers but were structurally suspect. Fokker claimed that his problems stemmed from an Albatros monopoly on the 160 hp Mercedes D.III engine, but the Fokker D.IV, at the bottom of this page, used this engine. The truth was less flattering; Fokker's early biplane fighter designs were inferior to the fighters from Albatros and Halberstadt. Although Fokker is justly famous for his *Eindeckers*, his later Triplane, the spectacular D.VII, and the innovative E.V/D.VIII, Fokker's D.I–D.V designs are nearly forgotten, and for good reason.

Above: The Fokker D.III was powered, like the earlier E.IV, by the 160 hp two-row Oberursel U.III. It carried two machine guns but its performance could not compare to the Albatros fighters. This is the first prototype; a small production run followed but the early Fokker biplane fighters did not last long at the front.

Left: Like the Albatros fighters, the Fokker D.IV was powered by the 160 hp Mercedes D.III, which Fokker claimed he could not get for his designs. The Fokker D.IV carried two machine guns but could not compete with the performance, maneuverability, or structural strength of the Albatros fighters.

Above: This photo of *Kest* 4b at Freiburg shows a first-generation Fokker E.IV fighter at left. Second-generation Fokker D.IIs are at the far end of the second row and the two closest fighters in the third row. Two second-generation Fokker D.III fighters are nearest the camera in the middle row. By far the best aircraft in the photo is the Halberstadt fighter furthest from the camera in the third row. The second-generation Fokker fighters, the D.I–D.V, are little-known due to their mediocrity compared to contemporary Halberstadt and Albatros fighters.

Below: Fokker D.II 54/16 waits for its next mission. The D.II used the 100 hp Oberursel U.I 9-cylinder rotary.

The Futility of Copying Bad Ideas

Impressed by the performance and maneuverability of the Nieuport sesquiplanes when compared to the Fokker *Eindeckers*, *Idflieg* circulated captured Nieuports to several manufacturers. Albatros copied the wing configuration for its D.III and Pfalz was influenced by the narrow-chord lower wing but used two spars in their D.III. However, Euler D.I basically copied the Nieuport 11. The SSW D.I was also a copy, but not as exact as that by Euler, and SSW used its own innovative engine for improved performance. The resulting D.I was as good or better than the Nieuport 17, but by the time it was ready for combat it was no longer competitive, demonstrating the futility of copying a bad idea and taking dead aim at a moving target.

Above: The SSW D.I was basically a copy of the Nieuport 17, but SSW used their own 110 hp Siemens-Halske Sh.I counter-rotary engine for better performance, which required a larger propeller. This early production model has no spinner.
Below: The spinner on this late-production SSW D.I gives it an aggressive look. The SSW D.I handled well but its performance was not competitive when it reached the front, which one would expect from copying an older design.

Above: The Euler D.I was basically a copy of the Nieuport 11. It was used only for training due to its limited performance.
Below: The AEG D.I owed nothing to the Nieuport and was a very fast, promising design. Powered by the same 160 hp Mercedes engine used in the Albatros fighters and mounting two machine guns, it climbed as well as the Albatros and reached 225 km/h (137 mph), making it the fastest fighter of its day. Three prototypes were built but after two unexplained fatal crashes, development was cancelled. Like all AEG designs its structure was welded steel tube.

Wickelrumpf

The Pfalz D.III used the *Wickelrumpf* technique of fuselage construction that Pfalz had learned from building the LFG Roland fighters under license. This entailed wrapping thin, narrow (50mm) strips of plywood around a mold and gluing them into a strong, light, monocoque shell. The photo below shows the wrapping process. During the late stages of the production process the fuselage was wrapped by a layer of fabric. Minimum framing was required. The technique facilitated streamlined shapes and conserved scarce resources by using abundant plywood. It also resisted battle damage because the entire shell carried the load, leaving no weak spots in the structure that could be disabled by a single bullet. Although labor intensive, this construction proved so successful that it was used in all subsequent Pfalz designs, including the Pfalz D.VIII, whose fuselage shells are shown ready for assembly in the photo at left.

A captured Pfalz D.III shows its structure. The fuselage shell was the main structure and required minimum framing.

Above: The Pfalz D.I was the Roland D.I built by Pfalz, and the Pfalz D.II was the Roland D.II built by Pfalz. This designation scheme was confusing, and soon *Idflieg* changed the designations of these aircraft to Roland D.I(Pfal) and Roland D.II(Pfal). Originally Pfalz was ordered to build the Roland D.III under license as the Pfalz D.III, but meanwhile Pfalz had developed their own original design, and testing soon revealed it was superior to the Roland D.III. Pfalz production was quickly changed to their own design, which appeared as the Pfalz D.III. Concerned about using a single-spar wing, Pfalz used a two-spar design for the lower wing of their D.III as shown by the interplane struts. The lower wing was still narrower in chord than the upper wing to provide the benefits of a better downward view, but without the fragility of the single-spar wing. The Pfalz D.III, the Albatros fighters, and the Roland D.I/II/III all used two guns and the same 160 hp Mercedes engine, and all had similar performance. The problem was the newer Allied fighters had better performance, creating a dilemma for the German fighter force from the summer of 1917. More powerful engines were key and Germany was slow to develop them, partly due to *Idflieg* complacency after Albatros fighters gained superiority in 1916.

Below: Like the Roland fighters that inspired it, the Pfalz D.III had its guns buried in the fuselage for better streamlining. Pilots soon complained that their lack of access to the guns in flight made it nearly impossible to clear jams and requested the guns be moved to the upper fuselage in front of the cockpit to solve the problem. Pfalz made the change, and the result was the Pfalz D.IIIa. At the same time, Pfalz extended the leading edge of the stabilizers to improve the ability to recover from a dive, and the tips of the lower wings were rounded to reduce in-flight vibration. Finally, most, perhaps all, D.IIIa fighters received the 180 hp Mercedes D.IIIa, a higher-compression version of the basic engine, to improve speed and climb. This same engine was also used in later production Albatros D.Va fighters and other designs.

Frontbeststand Inventory of Dr-Type Aircraft (Triplane Fighters) at the Front

	1914			1915						1916						1917						1918			
Manufacturer and Type	31 Aug	31 Oct	31 Dec	28 Feb	30 Apr	30 Jun	31 Aug	31 Oct	31 Dec	28 Feb	30 Apr	30 Jun	31 Aug	31 Oct	31 Dec	28 Feb	30 Apr	30 Jun	31 Aug	31 Oct	31 Dec	28 Feb	30 Apr	30 Jun	31 Aug
Fokker Dr.I																			2	17	35	143	171	118	65
Pfalz Dr.I																							9	7	1
Total:																			2	17	35	143	180	125	66

The Triplane Craze (Dr Types)

For sound structural and aerodynamic reasons, most airplanes before and during the war were either monoplanes or biplanes. However, in early 1917 Sopwith introduced a triplane development of their agile Pup fighter. The Sopwith Triplane retained the single gun and general lines of the Pup, but had a more powerful, 110 hp rotary coupled with a new triplane wing cellule. Although delicate and few in numbers, the Sopwith Triplane came as a nasty surprise to the dominant Albatros pilots because of the Allied fighters of the time it alone could out-climb the Albatros while also out-maneuvering it and matching it for speed. Despite the overall German superiority during the Spring of 1917, the Sopwith Triplane caused the Germans to think that perhaps the triplane configuration had some inherent superiority to the biplane. To the contrary, the biplane configuration is inherently a better compromise between strength, weight, and aerodynamic drag than the triplane, which has too much drag. However, the light, agile Sopwith

Triplane had hit a lucky peak of triplane potential, and the result was the 'triplane craze,' an affliction confined almost entirely to Germany and Austria.

Idflieg's response was misguided and inadequate. At first *Idflieg* asked German manufacturers to try the triplane configuration, and the triplane craze swept the German (and Austro-Hungarian) aviation industry. The triplane configuration was essentially a dead end, and *Idflieg's* request wasted a great deal of design resources. Of the multitude of triplanes designed, only two German triplane fighters reached production. One was the Pfalz Dr.I (Dr for *Dreidecker*, or triplane); only ten were built and while there are photographs of one at *Jasta 73*, its appearance in combat is not confirmed. The other was the Fokker Triplane, made famous as the airplane the Red Baron was flying when he was killed. Despite its fame, only 320 were built.

In many ways the Fokker Triplane is a paradox. It came at a time when the Albatros, Roland, and Pfalz fighters were inferior to their Allied opponents,

Left: *Lt.* Werner Voss in Fokker F.I 103/17, a pre-production prototype of the Fokker Dr.I, one of the iconic aircraft of WWI. This fame was partly due to the Red Baron being killed in his Fokker Triplane. Unfortunately, Voss met the same fate in a famous combat with No. 56 Squadron, RFC. The Triplane had great climb and maneuverability, but was slow. One innovation the Dr.I introduced was the airfoil over the axle between the wheels. The axle already created drag; the airfoil contributed lift as well. The undercarriage airfoil was a hallmark of later Fokker designs.

Above: The Pfalz Dr.II at left was a smaller, less powerful design based on the Pfalz Dr.I at right. Although a batch of ten Dr.Is, with the 160 hp Sh.III counter-rotary, was built, the Dr.II had lower performance and remained a single prototype.
Below: The AEG DJ.I triplane was an armored fighter designed to defend against Allied ground-attack aircraft at low alritudes where armor against rifle and machine-gun fire would be very useful for survivability. The DJ.I was too slow and a biplane version was then built and tested; it was faster but was not placed in production, perhaps due to the armistice.

Left: Pfalz Dr.I 3050/17 under test. Although the Pfalz Dr.I had the best climb of any WWI German aircraft, only ten were built. One reason was the engine was not yet fully ready for production; another was it was too slow.

Below: Although a triplane, this Roland fighter was designated the D.IV, not the Dr.I. This was the first Roland fighter to use the *klinkerrumpf* fuselage construction.

so was welcomed warmly by the German pilots. Initially beset with some structural failures due to poor quality control during production, the problems were soon rectified and it became a favorite mount of German aces despite being slow, its main limitation. On the positive side, it had exceptional climb and maneuverability ideally suited to close-in, high-G maneuvering combat, or dogfighting as it was called. It had the standard two synchronized machine guns and was, once the quality control problems were solved, a sturdy airplane. Despite the claims of some critics, it was not a copy of the Sopwith, sharing nothing in common with that airplane's design other than its

triplane configuration. While it needed more speed to be a first-class fighter, at least it out-performed its opponents in climb and maneuverability, whereas the Albatros was now inferior in all respects.

Eventually sanity prevailed, and designers abandoned the triplane configuration due to its higher drag. The Sopwith Triplane was replaced by the Camel biplane, which did not really out-perform it but was much sturdier and had two guns. The Fokker Triplane was developed into the Fokker D.VI biplane, which was faster. But the Fokker D.VII, of similar concept but powered by a water-cooled Mercedes or BMW, was a more potent fighter and D.VI production was limited.

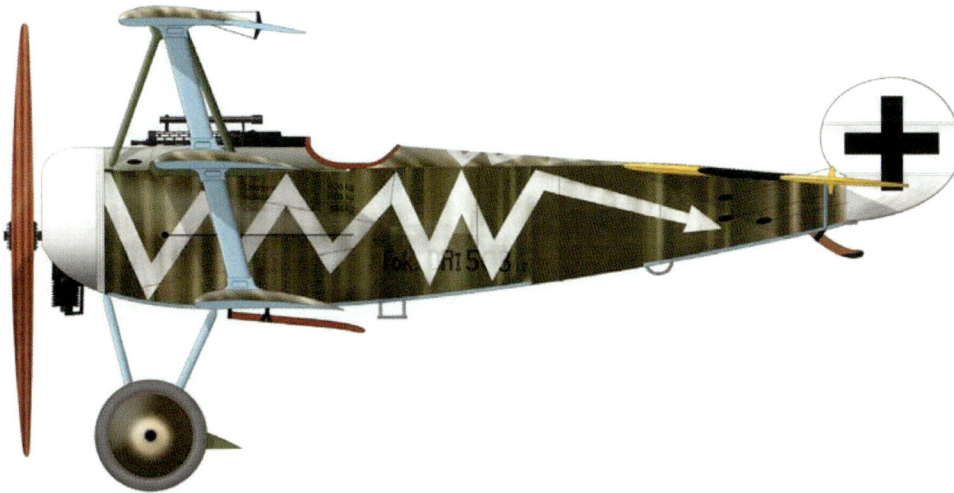

Fokker Dr.I 503/17 has the streaked factory camouflage finish with the *Jasta* 19 unit markings of white cowling and black and yellow stripes on the tailplane. Ace *Lt*. Hans Körner's personal marking is the white lightning bolt on the sides and turtledeck. Körner scored seven victories and survived the war.

Pfalz Dr.I 3050/17 is in factory finish with no unit or individual markings. The Pfalz factory finish evolved from overall silver-gray as seen here, which provided some camouflage in the air, to covering the flying surfaces in printed five-color camouflage fabric, to painting camouflage colors over the silver-gray fuselage.

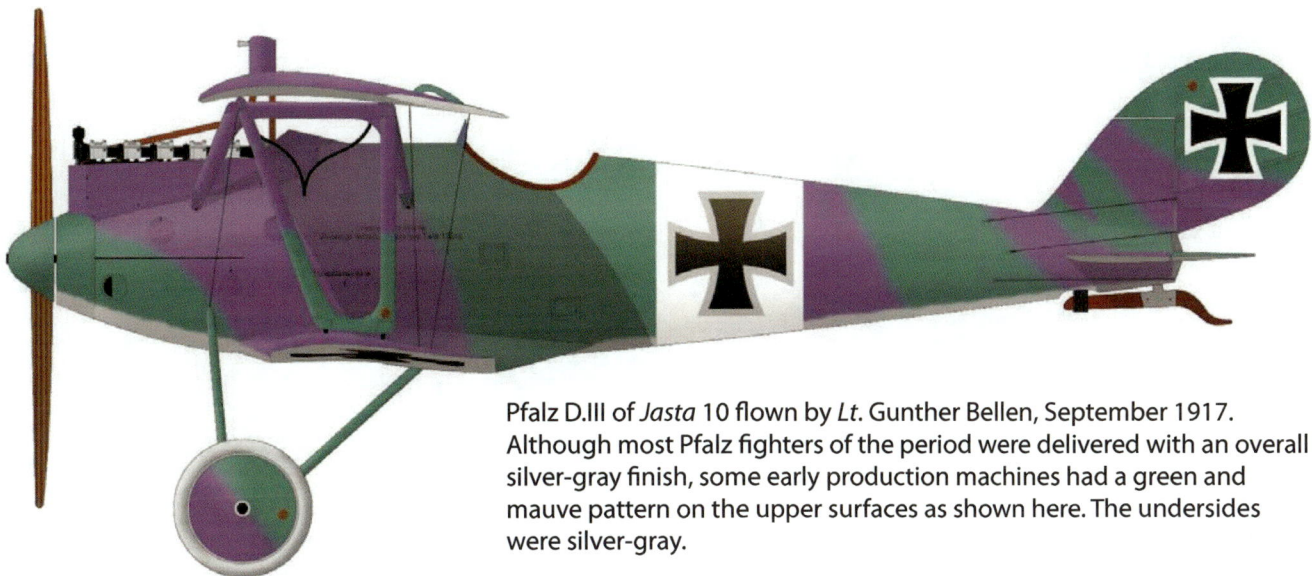

Pfalz D.III of *Jasta* 10 flown by *Lt*. Gunther Bellen, September 1917. Although most Pfalz fighters of the period were delivered with an overall silver-gray finish, some early production machines had a green and mauve pattern on the upper surfaces as shown here. The undersides were silver-gray.

Left: Even the Albatros D.V was fitted with a triplane wing cellule for comparison. The standard biplane D.V was faster, had better climb, and was more maneuverable due to the extra weight and drag of the triplane wings.

Left: During the German triplane craze, no biplane fighter was safe from modification. In addition to the Pfalz Dr.I and Dr.II designed from the beginning as triplanes, Pfalz also converted a standard D.III to a triplane. The standard biplane was faster, more maneuverable, and had better climb rate due to its lower drag.

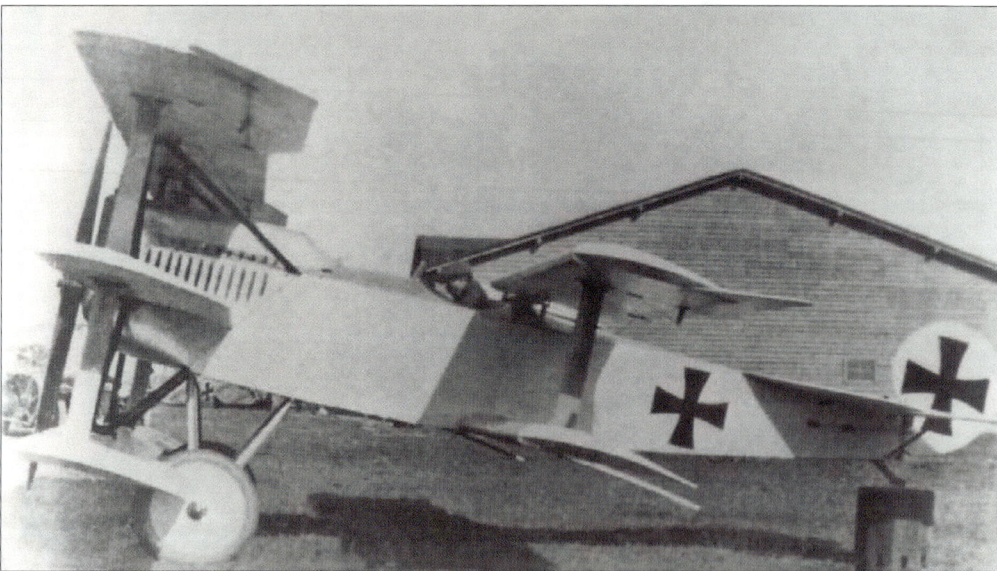

Above: The bizarre Fokker V8 prototype used a Triplane wing cellule in front and the upper two wings of a Triplane aft. Two short test flights proved the V8 had dangerous handling qualities and it was abandoned. WWI aircraft development was imperical, not theoretical, and the fact Fokker tried this five-wing monstrosity shows that the secret to his success was constant experimentation — many of which did not work!

Facing Page: The most famous airplane of WWI, this is the all-red Fokker Triplane in which the Red Baron was killed, almost certainly by ground fire, on 21 April 1918. The airplane, Dr.I 425/17, was painted red at the factory instead of the normal streaked camouflage Fokker used at the time, clearly indicating this aircraft was meant for the Red Baron.

Above & Right: Another bizarre triplane design was the SSW DDr.I. It used two 110 hp Sh.I engines, one mounted in front of the nacelle and the other mounted in the rear of the nacelle. The potential of this eccentric design remains unknown because it crashed on its first test flight before performance data could be recorded.

Left: The Schütte-Lanz company, which primarily built airships, also designed airplanes, but none reached production. Here is the Schütte-Lanz Dr.I, their entry into the triplane craze. Powered by a 160 hp Mercedes, it was out-performed by the similar Schütte-Lanz D.III biplane.

The *Amerika* Program

In addition to losing her technical superiority in late spring of 1917, Germany had other challenges, and chief among them was that America entered the war against her in April 1917. It was immediately clear that Germany would need to enlarge her air service to counter this new threat. In addition to enlarging the training establishment, Germany was forced to expand aircraft production to meet the challenge of America's entry into the war, and this became known as the *Amerika* Program. Key elements included:

- Increase aircraft production from 1,000 to 2,000 airplanes per month.
- Increase aero-engine production from 1,250 to 2,500 aero-engines per month.
- Increase aircraft machine-gun production to 1,500 per month.
- Increase aviation fuel output from 6,000 tons to 12,000 tons per month.
- Obtain 24,000 suitable recruits for the air service.
- Special effort to be joined to obtain technical superiority in aircraft, especially a new fighter plane and high-performance aero-engine.

Essentially, the *Amerika* Program aimed to double the output of combat airplanes and fuel, a goal never reached. See pages 130–132 for a detailed summary of planned production under the *Amerika* Program.

The German Fighter Competitions

Thus for a number of reasons – technical stagnation, largely due to engine stagnation, increasing Allied technical and numerical superiority, and American entry into the war making all these problems even more critical – German aviation was under great stress in late 1917.

At this time, Manfred von Richthofen, the 'Red Baron', Germany's leading ace famous throughout the Empire, contacted one of his junior officer friends on the *Idflieg* staff and complained strongly about the Albatros fighter. Richthofen suggested a fighter competition between all the German manufacturers to develop a superior new fighter. Such was his influence, and the common sense of the solution he recommended, that *Idflieg* decided to follow his suggestion, and the first German fighter competition was held in late January–early February 1918.

Although the competition was open to all designs, a winner was to be declared in two categories, one for aircraft powered by the existing 160 hp Mercedes D.III engine and one for rotary-powered fighters. In the Mercedes-engine category the modified Fokker V11 was selected for production as the Fokker D.VII. The Roland D.VIa was runner up, and an evaluation batch of 50 Roland D.VIa fighters was also ordered. Simultaneously, the semi-autonomous Bavarian authorities chose the Pfalz D.XII to replace the D.IIIa in production.

In the rotary-engine category the Fokker D.VI, powered by the readily-available 110 hp Oberursel U.II was chosen as one winner. Additionally, there was a new rotary engine in development, the innovative 160 hp Siemens-Halske Sh.III counter-rotary. Offering much more power than the

Right: The Roland D.V biplane fighter did not go into production.

Below: The elegant Pfalz D.VI, powered by a 110 hp Oberursel Ur.II rotary, did not go into production despite its good maneuverability and flying qualities. The reason for this is not known but possibly was connected with the general shortage of lubricants for rotary engines in Germany. It appeared in January 1917, when the Albatros reigned supreme, and that may have been the real reason it was not built.

Oberursel, the Sh.III powered prototypes from SSW and Pfalz, and evaluation batches of both the SSW D.III and Pfalz D.VIII were ordered.

The key result was the selection of a superior fighter, the Fokker D.VII, to replace the outdated Albatros and Pfalz fighters. Significantly, the D.VII was initially powered by the same Mercedes engine used in those fighters, but finally a new engine, the over-compressed 185 hp BMW III became available, enabling more of the airframe's potential to be exploited. Mercedes responded with improved versions of their basic engine offering similar performance. The resulting BMW-powered fighter is thought by many, including the author, to be the finest all-around fighter of the war.

Two subsequent fighter competitions were held. The second, in May–June 1918, resulted in production of the Fokker E.V/D.VIII, a parasol-monoplane derivative of the Fokker Dr.I and D.VI. The Fokker V.29, a parasol-monoplane derivative of the Fokker D.VII, won the third fighter competition in October 1918 and would have gone into production except for the armistice. The third competition was restricted to fighters with BMW. IIIa engines, although several rotary-powered fighters were included for comparison. The Rumpler D.I was also chosen, but was not ready for production before the armistice.

German Fighter Aircraft Competing at the First Fighter Competition (D *Flugzeug Wettbewerb*) Held at Adlershof during January–February 1918

Aircraft	Engine
A.E.G. D.I*	Mercedes D.III
Albatros D.Va 7117/17	B.M.W.IIIa
Albatros D.Va (factory #4563)	Mercedes D.IIIaü (high compression)
Albatros D.Va 7089/17	Mercedes D.III
Albatros D.Va 7090/17	Mercedes D.III
Aviatik D.III	Benz Bz.IIIb (high speed)
Fokker V.9*	Oberursel U.II
Fokker V.11	Mercedes D.III
Fokker V.13-I	Oberursel U.III
Fokker V.13-II	Siemens-Halske Sh.III
Fokker V.17	Oberursel U.II
Fokker V.18	Mercedes D.III
Fokker V.20*	Mercedes D.III
Fokker Dr.I 201/17	Goebel Goe.III
Fokker Dr.I 469/17	Oberursel U.III
Kondor D.II*	Oberursel U.II
Pfalz D.IIIa 5935/17	Mercedes D.III
Pfalz D.IIIa 6033/17	Mercedes D.III
Pfalz D.VI	Oberursel U.II
Pfalz D.VII	Siemens-Halske Sh.III
Roland D.VI	Benz Bz.IIIa
Roland D.VI	Mercedes D.III
Roland D.VII*	Mercedes D.III
Roland D.IX	Siemens-Halske Sh.III
Rumpler D (U-strut)	Mercedes D.III
Rumpler D (parallel-strut)	Mercedes D.III
Schütte-Lanz D.III	Mercedes D.III
Siemens-Schuckert D.III 8340/17	Siemens-Halske Sh.III

The Roland D.IX biplane fighter prototype was powered by the Siemens-Halske Sh.III.

Notes:
1. An * indicates not listed in the official flight result tabulations, but present without competing.
2. The Fokker V11 won the competition and became the prototype for the production Fokker D.VII.
3. Small numbers of the Roland D.VI were ordered for operational evaluation at the Front.
4. Small numbers of the Fokker D.VI, the production version of the Fokker V.13, were ordered for operational evaluation at the Front.
5. Both the Pfalz D.VII and SSW D.III powered by the 160 hp Siemens-Halske Sh.III demonstrated excellent climb. The Pfalz D.VIII, a stronger, two-bay derivative of the D.VII, was ordered along with the SSW D.III for operational evaluation at the Front.
6. Because Pfalz was a Bavarian company and Bavaria wanted to maintain as much autonomy as possible, the Pfalz D.XII replaced the Pfalz D.IIIa in production despite not being at the competition.

Siemens-Halske Rotary Engine

Two aircraft powered by an innovative counter-rotary engine made a good impression at the First Fighter Competition and saw operational service limited primarily by engine availability. These were the Pfalz D.VIII and Siemens-Schuckert D.III, both powered by the 160 hp Siemens-Halske Sh.III rotary. In this unique engine the cylinders rotated in one direction while the propeller rotated in the other, giving a relative speed of 1,800 rpm with a propeller speed of only 900 rpm. Compared to a typical rotary of 1,400 rpm, this enabled the Sh.III to produce more power while allowing use of a larger, slower-turning, and more efficient propeller, giving the fighters good speed and exceptional climb. The SSW D.III was used in small numbers before being replaced with the similar D.IV, which was faster due to reduced drag from a smaller wing. The Pfalz D.VIII was not as maneuverable as the SSW fighters but had similar climb, so most were assigned to the KESTs (*Kampeinsitzer Staffeln*) stationed behind the lines to intercept Allied day bombers.

Fokker's Triumph – the D.VII

Fokker had struggled since the eclipse of his *Eindeckers,* and his famous but slow Triplane was only a partial success. Limited to the same engines and guns his competitors used, Fokker needed a significant innovation to built a dramatically better airplane, and he finally achieved it in the Fokker D.VII with its wing of innovative structural and aerodynamic design. Constant experimentation was key to his success.

Above: One of the greatest services Manfred von Richthofen did for Germany was instigating the fighter competitions, and the Fokker D.VII was the greatest result of those competitions. Arriving at the front days after Richthofen's death in his Fokker Triplane, he was not able to fly the D.VII in combat himself. Initially using the Mercedes D.IIIa engine, when fitted with the superb 185 hp BMW.IIIa it was the best all-around fighter of the war. This D.VII flew with *Jasta* 49.

Although sharing its engine and armament with the Albatros, Pfalz, and other German designs, the Fokker D.VII introduced some important structural and aerodynamic innovations that greatly improved its effectiveness. By far the most important was its thick wooden wing built around a box spar. The thick wing, with its rounded leading edge, offered high lift and exceptional stalling characteristics, making the D.VII maneuverable and easy to fly, and enabling it to fly 'hanging on its prop' without stalling. These exceptional handling qualities made good pilots out of average ones and made aces out of good pilots. Other designers used thin airfoils because they had somewhat less drag than the thick Fokker wing. However, the strong Fokker wing eliminated the need for the extensive system of bracing wires that thin airfoils required. The combined drag of thin airfoils with their bracing wires was significantly more than the drag of the thick Fokker wing which needed no bracing wires, and this was the secret to the Fokker's improved speed and climb with the same power.

Due to stagnant engine development, upon its introduction to service the Fokker D.VII was powered by the same 160 hp Mercedes D.III engine used in the Albatros scouts in August 1916! It was not until the new BMW engine finally arrived in June/July that the Fokker D.VII fulfilled its full potential and became the premier fighter of the war. The BMW engine was similar to the familiar 160 hp Mercedes D.III engine but developed its 185 hp at 2,000 meters altitude because it was over-compressed. That meant it could not be run at full throttle until reaching the thinner air at 2,000 meters without detonation and engine damage. This design gave it more power at high altitude for increased speed and exceptional climb. Mercedes countered with the 180 hp D.IIIa and finally the 200 hp D.IIIaü, the latter being over-compressed like the BMW. Both engines were used in the D.VII, with the D.IIIaü giving performance equivalent to the BMW. Although the BMW-powered Fokker D.VII became a legend in its own time, there were never enough of them to win the air war for Germany.

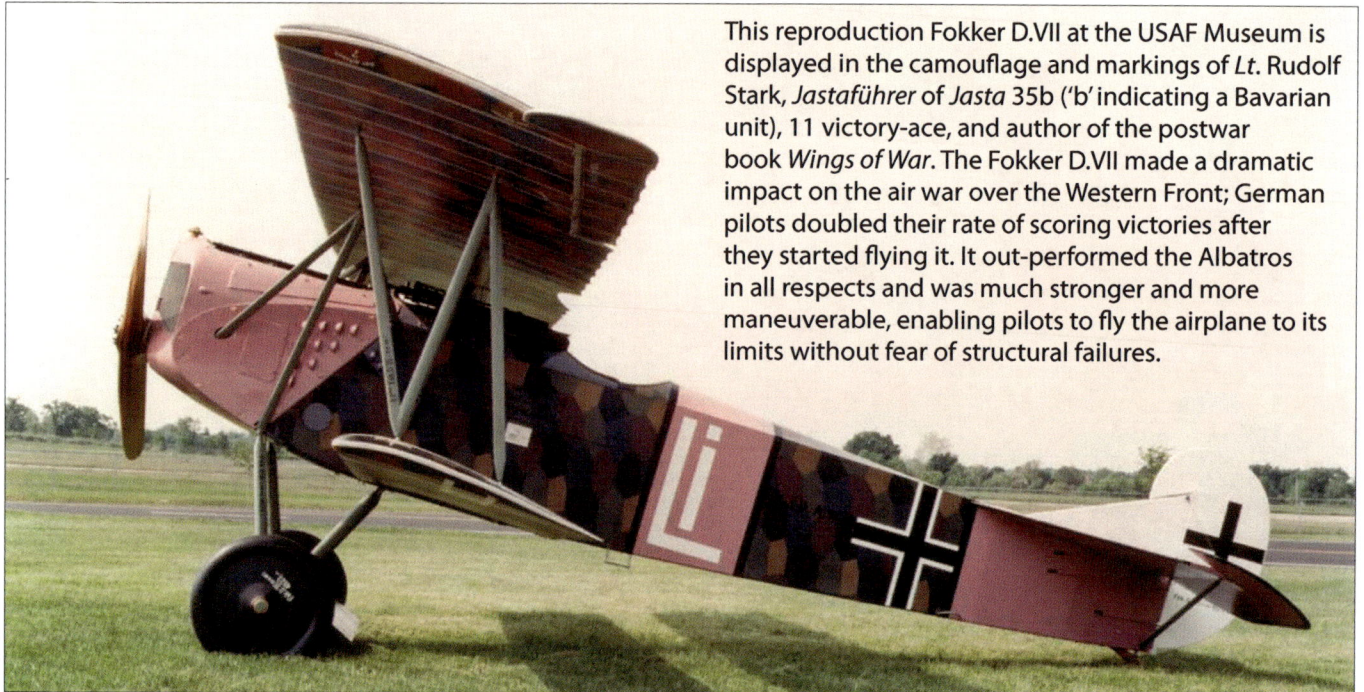

This reproduction Fokker D.VII at the USAF Museum is displayed in the camouflage and markings of *Lt.* Rudolf Stark, *Jastaführer* of *Jasta* 35b ('b' indicating a Bavarian unit), 11 victory-ace, and author of the postwar book *Wings of War*. The Fokker D.VII made a dramatic impact on the air war over the Western Front; German pilots doubled their rate of scoring victories after they started flying it. It out-performed the Albatros in all respects and was much stronger and more maneuverable, enabling pilots to fly the airplane to its limits without fear of structural failures.

This Fokker D.VII, flown by *Lt.* Richard Kraut of *Jasta* 66, was brought to Canada as war booty after the armistice; his initials are painted on the red fuselage band.

Fratz was a Fokker D.VI serving with *Jasta* 80b; it was flown by *Lt.* Seit. The aircraft is in factory finish with name, black fuselage band, and white outlines added at *Jasta* 80b.

Above: Powered by the innovative 160 hp Siemens-Halske Sh.III counter-rotary engine, the Pfalz D.VII looked like a biplane conversion of the earlier Pfalz Dr.I. The oil-streaked cowling indicates the engine needs further development!
Below: The Pfalz D.VIII was a two-bay version of the D.VII. The extra struts made it stronger, so it was selected for production, but their additional weight and drag reduced speed and climb compared to the D.VII. Here ace Paul Baümer stands in front of his early-production D.VIII while serving with *Jasta* Boelcke. Eventually development work on the single-bay D.VII enabled it to go into production, but none reached the front before the armistice.

Left & Below: The SSW D.III was powered by the same 160 hp Siemens-Halske Sh.III used in the Pfalz D.VIII; the SSW D.III had similar performance but was more maneuverable than the D.VIII. These photos show an early production SSW D.III in service with *Jasta* 19. Fokker Triplanes are lined up in the background. The SSW D.III was subject to constant small changes to improve maneuverability and engine reliability.

Right: Although the SSW D.III offered exceptional climb and ceiling, pilots wanted more speed. The D.III was modified into the similar D.IV by reducing the upper wing chord to reduce weight and drag; speed was improved by 10 km/h at the cost of a slight reduction in climb rate. Here D.IVs are in *Jasta* service. The interplane struts taper closer together on the upper wing than on the D.III due to the reduced chord.

Pfalz D.VIII flown by Paul Bäumer while serving with *Jasta* Boelcke in May 1918. The white tail (black on the other side) and black and white nose stripes are the *Jasta* markings. The red/white/black chevron in German national colors was Bäumer's personal marking. The silver-gray fuselage and wings covered with five-color printed camouflage fabric were the standard factory finish when this aircraft was built. *Lt.* Bäumer scored 43 victories, was awarded the *Pour le Mérite*, and survived the war.

SSW D.III flown by *Lt.* Ernst Udet. The red colors and "Lo!" on the fuselage side are Udet's personal markings. Udet scored 62 victories, second only to the Red Baron among German aces, was awarded the *Pour le Mérite*, and survived the war to become a famous stunt pilot between the wars.

SSW D.IV of *Jasta* 12. The blue fuselage and white nose were the *Jasta* markings. The D.IV had a narrower chord upper wing than the D.III for increased speed. The exceptional climb and maneuverability of the SSW fighters enabled them to intercept high-flying reconnaissance airplanes and fighters. Their pilots thought them the best fighters of the war, but they served in small numbers due to the prolonged teething troubles of their innovative engine.

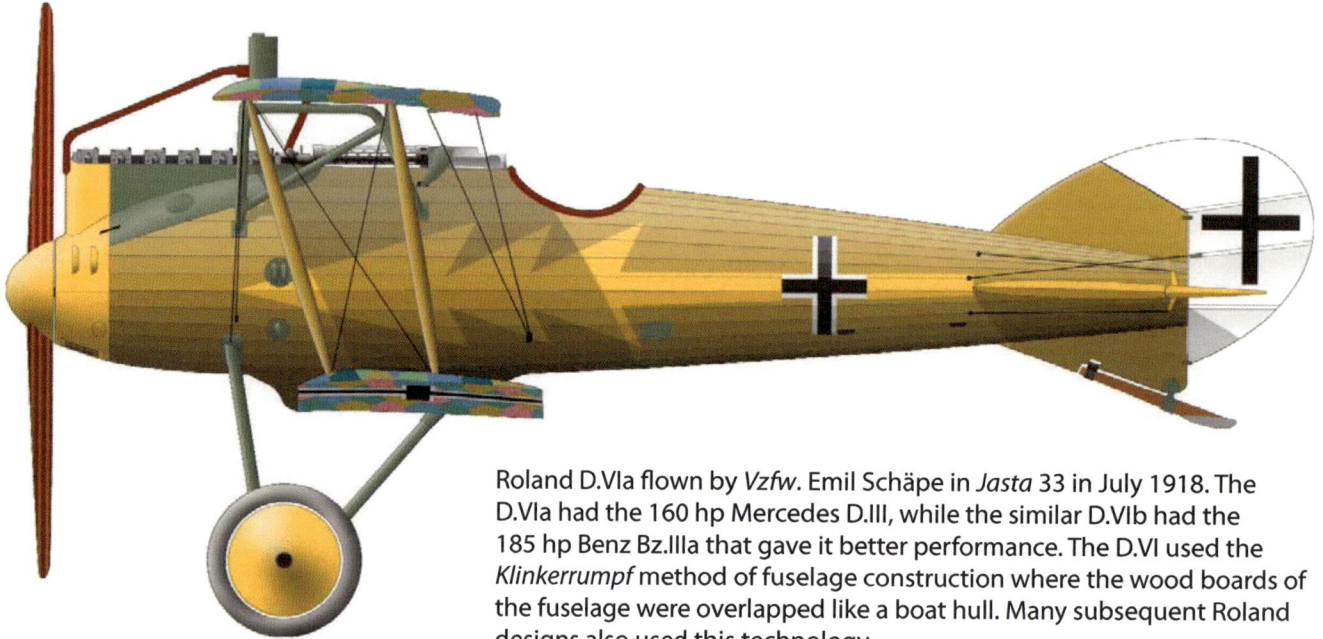

Roland D.VIa flown by *Vzfw.* Emil Schäpe in *Jasta* 33 in July 1918. The D.VIa had the 160 hp Mercedes D.III, while the similar D.VIb had the 185 hp Benz Bz.IIIa that gave it better performance. The D.VI used the *Klinkerrumpf* method of fuselage construction where the wood boards of the fuselage were overlapped like a boat hull. Many subsequent Roland designs also used this technology.

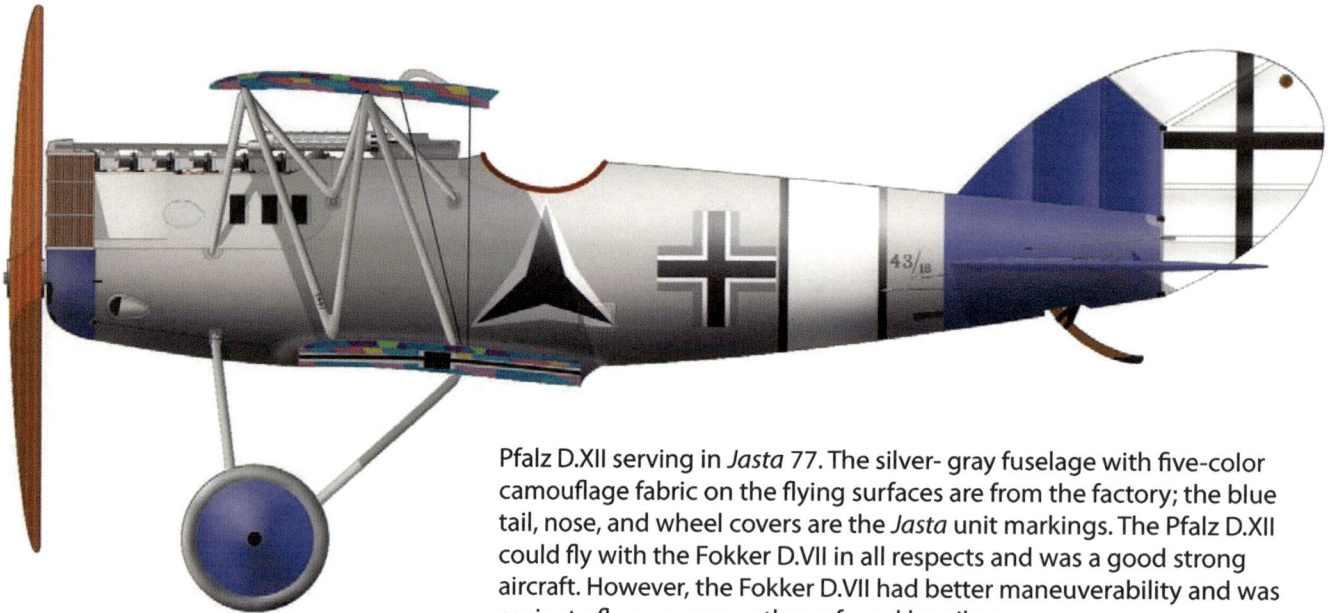

Pfalz D.XII serving in *Jasta* 77. The silver- gray fuselage with five-color camouflage fabric on the flying surfaces are from the factory; the blue tail, nose, and wheel covers are the *Jasta* unit markings. The Pfalz D.XII could fly with the Fokker D.VII in all respects and was a good strong aircraft. However, the Fokker D.VII had better maneuverability and was easier to fly, so was greatly preferred by pilots.

Original Fokker D.VII on display at the Knowlton Museum in Canada.

Above: Although the Roland D.VI did not win the First Fighter Competition, it made a good enough showing that 50 were ordered for operational evaluation at the front. This spectacular example was flown by *Pour le Mérite* ace Otto Kissenberth with *Jasta* 23b. A good fighter, the Roland D.VI was overshadowed by the Fokker D.VII.

Below: The Fokker D.VI was a smaller, lighter version of the D.VII powered by a 110 hp Oberursel. This one is serving with *Jasta* 80b. Somewhat more maneuverable than the larger D.VII and slightly faster at low altitude, the low-powered rotary limited the D.VI to production of only 120 aircraft. Because most rotaries lost power with altitude faster than inline engines – the exceptions being the Siemens-Halske Sh.III and Sh.IIIa – the more powerful inline engines in the D.VII gave it better performance at higher altitudes, where most combats were fought by 1918.

Second Fighter Competition May–June 1918

Aircraft	Engine
Albatros D.X 2206/18 (#4914)	Benz Bz.IIIb o (un-geared)
Albatros D.XI 2209/18 (#5045)	Siemens-Halske Sh.III
Aviatik D.III 3550/18 (#10012)	Benz Bz.IIIb o (un-geared)
Aviatik D.III (Versuch)(#10005)	Benz Bz.IIIb o (un-geared)
Aviatik D.IV (#10008)	Benz Bz.IIIb v
Daimler D.I (#60)	Mercedes D.IIIb v (high speed)
Fokker V21 (#2310)	Mercedes D.IIIü (high-compression)
Fokker V23 (#2443)	Mercedes D.III
Fokker V24 (#2612)	Benz Bz.IVü (high-compression)
Fokker V25 (#2732)	Oberursel U.II
Fokker V27 (#2734)	Benz Bz.IIIb o ü (un-geared)
Fokker V28 (#2735)	Oberursel U.II
Fokker V28 (#2735)	Oberursel U.III
Fokker V28 (#2735)	Goebel Goe.III
Fokker D.VII [#2268]	Mercedes D.III
Fokker D.VII (Alb.) 527/18 (#5148)	Mercedes D.III
Junkers J.9	Mercedes D.IIIü (high-compression)
Kondor D.I (#200)	Oberursel U.II
Kondor D.II (#201)	Oberursel U.II
LVG D.IV	Benz Bz.IIIb o
Pfalz D.VIII 150/18	Siemens-Halske Sh.III (Rh)
Pfalz D.VIII 158/18	Oberursel U.III
Pfalz D.XII 1375/18	Mercedes D.IIIaü (high-compression)
Pfalz D.XII 1387/18	B.M.W.IIIa
Pfalz D.XIIa	Benz Bz.IIIoü (high-compression)
Pfalz D.XIV	Benz Bz.IVü (high-compression)
Roland D.VIb	Benz Bz.IIIaü (high-compression)
Roland D.VII 224/18 (#3780)	Benz Bz.IIIb o (un-geared)
Roland D.IX 3001/18 (#3900)	Siemens-Halske Sh.III
Rumpler D.I 1552/18	Mercedes D.III
Rumpler D.I 1553/18 (#4402)	Mercedes D.III
Schütte-Lanz D.VII/3	Mercedes D.IIIü (high-compression)
Siemens-Schukert D.III 1627/18	Siemens-Halske Sh.III
Siemens-Schukert D.III 1629/18	Siemens-Halske Sh.III
Siemens-Schukert D.III 3008/18	Siemens-Halske Sh.III
Siemens-Schukert D.IIIa 1622/18	Siemens-Halske Sh.III
Siemens-Schukert D.V 7557/17	Siemens-Halske Sh.III

Notes:
1. Numbers in parentheses are factory numbers.
2. Fokker D.VII #2268; the #2268 may be factory or military number.
3. One of the Rumpler D.I fighters was also flown with a Mercedes D.IIIaü (high-compression).
4. The Fokker V.26 won the competition and, slightly modified, was placed into production as the Fokker E.V.

Below Left: Powered by the 200 hp Benz Bz.IVü, the Pfalz D.XIV was an enlarged D.XII.
Below: Schütte-Lanz D.VII.

Fighter Evaluation Flights by Front-Line Pilots, Adlershof, July 1918

These flights were an adjunct to the Second Fighter Competition, and included some additional aircraft (noted by an *) that had not participated in the competition.

Aircraft	Engine
Albatros D.X 2206/18 (#4914)	Benz Bz.IIIb o (un-geared)
Albatros D.XII 2210/18*	Mercedes D.III
Aviatik D.III 3550/18 (#10012)	Benz Bz.IIIb o (un-geared)
Aviatik D.III (Versuch)(#10005)	Benz Bz.IIIb o (un-geared)
Aviatik D.IV (#10008)	Benz Bz.IIIb v
Aviatik D.VI*	Benz Bz.IIIb m. (geared)
Daimler D.I (#60)	Mercedes D.IIIb v (high speed)
Fokker V24 (#2612)	Benz Bz.IVü (high-compression)
Fokker V27 (#2734)	Benz Bz.IIIb o ü (un-geared)
Fokker V27 (#2734)*	Benz Bz.IIIb m. (geared)
Fokker V28 (#2735)	Oberursel U.II
Fokker V28 (#2735)	Oberursel U.III
Fokker D.VII*	B.M.W.IIIa
Fokker D.VII*	Mercedes D.III
Fokker D.VII (Alb.) 527/18 (#5148)	Mercedes D.III
Fokker D.VII (Oaw.)*	Mercedes D.III
Junkers D.I	Mercedes D.III
Kondor D.I (#200)	Oberursel U.II
Kondor D.II (#201)	Oberursel U.II
Naglo D.II 1165/18*	Mercedes D.III
Pfalz D.VIII 150/18	Siemens-Halske Sh.III (Rh)
Pfalz D.VIII 158/18	Oberursel U.III
Pfalz Parasol (D.X)*	Siemens-Halske Sh.III
Pfalz D.XII 1371/18*	Mercedes D.IIIaü (high-compression)
Pfalz D.XII 1387/18	B.M.W.IIIa
Pfalz D.XIIa	Benz Bz.IIIoü (high-compression)
Pfalz D.XIV	Benz Bz.IVü (high-compression)
Roland D.VIb [2225]*	Benz Bz.IIIav
Roland D.VII 224/18 (#3780)	Benz Bz.IIIb o (un-geared)
Roland D.VII*	Benz Bz.IIIb m. (geared)
Roland D.IX 3001/18 (#3900)	Siemens-Halske Sh.III
Roland D.XIV 3002/18*	Goebel Goe.III
Rumpler D.I 1552/18	Mercedes D.III
Rumpler D.I 1553/18 (#4402)	Mercedes D.III
Schütte-Lanz D.VII/3	Mercedes D.IIIü (high-compression)
Siemens-Schukert D.III 1627/18	Siemens-Halske Sh.III
Siemens-Schukert D.III 1629/18	Siemens-Halske Sh.III
Siemens-Schukert D.IIIa 1622/18	Siemens-Halske Sh.III
Siemens-Schukert D.IV 7555/17*	Siemens-Halske Sh.III
Siemens-Schukert D.V 7557/17	Siemens-Halske Sh.III
Zeppelin D.I*	Mercedes D.III

The all-metal Zeppelin D.I.

Notes:

1. *Lt.* Reinhard (JGI) was killed 3 July 1918 when the top wing of the Zeppelin D.I tore off.

Above: The Kondor D.II.
Left: The Junkers D.I was the world's first all-metal fighter.

Above: The Fokker V26, which became the E.V, won the Second Fighter Competition despite the low power of its 110 hp Oberursel. This spectacular example was flown by *Jasta* 6 in August 1918 until a series of fatal accidents were attributed to poor assembly and quality control at the factory. The E.V had to be withdrawn for wing replacement. By the time the planes returned to the front in October, *Idflieg* had decided that all fighters would be in the 'D' category and the E.V was re-designated the Fokker D.VIII. The E.V/D.VIII represented the simplest fighter that could be built.

Below: The German state of Bavaria wanted to maintain as much autonomy as possible within Imperial Germany and one manifestation of that desire was its support of the Pfalz company, located in Bavaria. Pfalz built airplanes throughout the war, initially license-built copies of the Morane-Saulnier L, and later original fighter designs. The Pfalz D.III was a good, solid fighter that just needed more power to be competitive with Allied fighters. The Pfalz D.XII looked similar to the Fokker D.VII and went into service in the summer of 1918; problems with its frontal, car-type radiator delayed its arrival by a couple of months. By the time the D.XII arrived the Fokker D.VII had a huge reputation and was in great demand by the pilots, most of whom wanted nothing else. The D.XII was another good, solid Pfalz design over-shadowed by its competition that never made a name for itself. But one manifestation of Bavaria's desire for autonomy exists today; the BMW company, which was created from the old Bavarian Rapp engine company in 1917. The Pfalz D.XII below is an early production example; later production aircraft had a rounded fin and rudder. Power was the Mercdes D.IIIa/av/avü series.

Fokker E.V in factory finish except for its red cowling. Powered by the 110 hp Oberursel U.II of 1915, the E.V was the simplest fighter aircraft Fokker could design. Despite the low power performance was good, but poor manufacturing quality lead to fatal wing failures and the aircraft soon had to be withdrawn for new wings.

Production Pfalz D.XV in factory finish. The D.XV, a 'wireless' development of the D.XII, was at the *flugparks* the last week of the war but did not reach combat. The D.XV was considered the equal in performance, maneuverability, and flying characteristics of the famous D.VII, but never had the opportunity to prove itself. It was forgotten and after the war Pfalz went bankrupt. Power was the 185 hp BMW.IIIa engine.

Left: Another view of the USAF Museum's replica Fokker D.VII in the markings of *Lt.* Rudolf Stark, *Jastaführer* of *Jasta* 35b. The aircraft is in standard factory finish of overall camouflage fabric with Stark's lilac personal markings. The pink lines over the wing ribs were colored fabric strips used to sew the wing fabric securely to the ribs to maintain the airfoil section. Pink, blue, and camouflage fabric were all used to sew ribs.

Third Fighter Competition, October 1918

This Competition was officially restricted to fighters with B.M.W. IIIa engines, but as may be seen from reviewing the list of participants, several rotary-engined types were included for comparison.

Aircraft	Engine
Albatros D.XI	Siemens-Halske Sh.III
Albatros D.XII	B.M.W.IIIa
Fokker V.28	Siemens-Halske Sh.III
Fokker V.29	B.M.W.IIIa
Fokker V.36	B.M.W.IIIa
Fokker D.VIII	Oberursel U.III
Junkers D.I	B.M.W.IIIa
Kondor E.III	Oberursel U.III
Kondor E.IIIa	Goebel Goe.III
Pfalz D.XVf	B.M.W.IIIa
Pfalz D.XV (special)	B.M.W.IIIa
Roland D.XVI	Siemens-Halske Sh.III
Roland D.XVII	B.M.W.IIIa
Rumpler D.I	B.M.W.IIIa
Zeppelin D.I	B.M.W.IIIa

Above: The Roland D.XVI powered by the 160 hp Sh.III. By late 1918 German army fighter prototypes were often monoplanes, as were all naval two-seat floatplane fighter prototypes.

Notes:

1. Pilots participating: von Schleich (*JG* IV), Bongartz, (*Jasta* 36) Mohnicke, Jacobs (*Jasta* 7), Udet (*Jasta* 4), Veltjens (*Jasta* 15), Baumer (*Jasta* Boelcke), von Bonigk (*JG* II), Lothar von Richthofen, Lorzer (*JG* III), von Billow (*Idflieg*), Thuy (*Jasta* 28), Blume (*Jasta* 9).
2. Two aircraft were selected as winners of the Third Fighter Competition, the Fokker V.29 and Rumpler D.I.

Above: The Fokker V29 shown here was one of the two winners of the Third Fighter Competition. Essentially, it was a parasol monoplane derivative of the Fokker D.VII. Similar to the smaller D.VIII, it had the more powerful 185 hp BMW. IIIa engine instead of a rotary for better high altitude performance. Similarly, the more powerful D.VII had eclipsed the smaller, rotary-powered D.VI of similar configuration.

Above: The other winner of the Third Fighter Competition was the Rumpler D.I, which offered exceptional ceiling and high-altutide performance. Rumpler struggled for a long time with its prolonged development and it was too late for combat; it might have gained a good reputation had it arrived in time. Prototypes used the Mercedes D.IIIa engine, but the production aircraft specified use of the 185 hp BMW.IIIa engine for superior climb and ceiling.

Above: The Pfalz D.XV, finally with the 185 hp BMW.IIIa engine the D.XII had needed to reach its full potential, was an excellent fighter developed from the D.XII. It was as fast and maneuverable as the Fokker D.VII, and the first examples arrived at the Army *Flugparks* the last week of the war. Missing combat, it was forgotten in the war's aftermath.

Bombers

Twin-Engine Bombers (G Types)

Early in the war Germany pursued the 'Kampfflugzeug' or battleplane concept, which lead to development of the twin-engine AEG K.I, the 'K' standing for 'Kampfflugzeug'. The Kampfflugzeug was envisioned as a sort of aerial cruiser with gunners engaging enemy aircraft with flexible guns analogous to naval combat. Operational experience quickly revealed that the slow Kampfflugzeug was better suited to bombing than intercepting aircraft and the designation of the AEG K.I was changed to AEG G.I, 'G' standing for 'Grossflugzeug', literally 'large aircraft' but in this case also having the connotation of twin-engine bomber. AEG were first to field G-types, soon followed by Gotha, then Rumpler, Friedrichshafen, and Albatros.

Both the Rumpler and Albatros designs were mediocre and built in very small numbers. Contrary to the Frontbestand, the Albatros G.II remained a prototype. Only the Albatros G.III was produced and served at the front, and the inventory of G.II aircraft were actually Albatros G.III aircraft; the numbers in the two rows should be combined under G.III.

The Gotha went on to fame for bombing London in broad daylight in June 1917, and later switched to night bombing after British defenses were greatly strengthened, then bombed tactical targets behind Allied lines during and after the great German offensive in March 1918. The AEG G-types were successful tactical bombers from their appearance at the front. The AEG G.IV listed in December 1915 was a transcription error; the G.IV did not reach the front until 1917. Friedrichshafen G-types were also successful, both they and the AEG series both being superior to the Gotha in all respects except range and ceiling. In early 1918 Gotha abandoned their existing designs in favor of smaller, faster designs, but despite prolonged development these did not reach the front.

The G-types were very effective tactical night bombers and the armistice specifically required the Germans to surrender all G-types to the Allies, who were astonished at the small number of aircraft they received given the damage they had done. Resource shortages, especially engines, limited the number of G-types Germany could build.

Above: For its role in bombing London by day in June 1917, the Gotha G.IV became by far the most famous German bomber of the war. G.IV 408/16 was one of those raiders and here is being postioned by a ground crew.

Frontbeststand Inventory of G-Type Aircraft (Twin-Engine Bombers) at the Front

Manufacturer and Type	1914 31 Aug	31 Oct	31 Dec	1915 28 Feb	30 Apr	30 Jun	31 Aug	31 Oct	31 Dec	1916 28 Feb	30 Apr	30 Jun	31 Aug	31 Oct	31 Dec	1917 28 Feb	30 Apr	30 Jun	31 Aug	31 Oct	31 Dec	1918 28 Feb	30 Apr	30 Jun	31 Aug
AEG G.I							1	5			5														
AEG G.II						2	5	10	13	12	2	4	4	4	2	2	1	1							
AEG G.III												6	16	22	21	22	9								
AEG G.IV									1								5	9	15	15	35	37	54	74	51
AEG G.																	3								
Albatros G.II																1	9	1	1		1				
Albatros G.III																	2	1	2						
Friedrichshafen G.II														1		4	8	17	17	10	9	2	1	1	1
Friedrichshafen G.III																		9	32	24	57	69	96	74	24
Friedrichshafen G.IIIa																								18	95
Friedrichshafen G.IV																								4	8
Friedrichshafen G.IVa																								5	6
Gotha G.I								5	6	1		1	1	1											
Gotha G.II														4	3	1	1								
Gotha G.III														7	14	3	4	3	3						
Gotha G.IV															1		30	36	34	35	19	10	8	6	5
Gotha G.V																			3	20	33	34	36	15	8
Gotha G.Va																							11	19	4
Gotha G.Vb																									21
Rumpler G.I												1		1											
Rumpler G.II												1	7	8	4	1	1								
Rumpler G.III															1		3	5	5	10	1	4			
Total:						2	6	20	20	13	7	13	28	48	46	34	71	86	111	116	155	156	206	216	223

Above: Designed by Ursinus and built by Gotha, this aircraft became the Gotha G.I and started Gotha in the bomber business. Subsequent Gotha designs bore no relationship to the G.I.

Above: The Gotha G.II set the basic design followed by all subsequent Gotha bombers operational during the war.

The Gotha G.III shown here was an intermediate step between Gotha's original G.II design and the G.IV that bombed London in daylight in June 1917.

One of the Gotha G.IV bombers that bombed London in daylight. Engines were the the 260 hp Mercedes D.IVa

Above: This Gotha G.IV participated in the daylight bombing raids over London in 1917.

Above: The Gotha G.V had revised engine nacelles that were supported above the lower wing on struts. Performance was little improved over the G.IV because both used the same engines and basic airframe. Improved British defenses meant the G.V was used for night bombing over the UK and later for tactical bombing over the Western Front.

B.1092/14

The Friedel-Ursinus was built at *Flieger Ersatz Abteilung* 3 and became the prototype for the Gotha G.I. The pilot sat in the rear cockpit with the two gunners in separate cockpits in front of him. Designed as a *Kampfflugzeug*, or battle plane, it was more effective as a bomber.

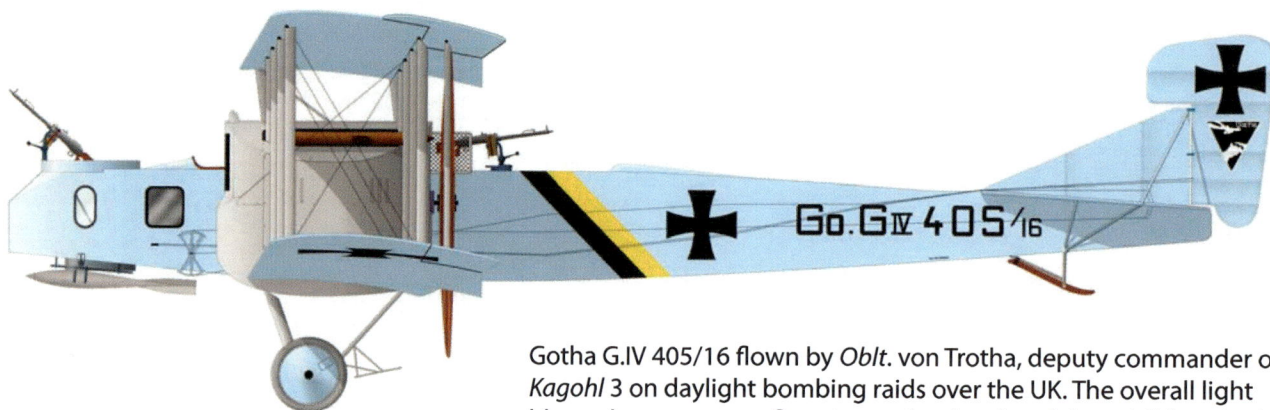

Go.GIV 405/16

Gotha G.IV 405/16 flown by *Oblt*. von Trotha, deputy commander of *Kagohl* 3 on daylight bombing raids over the UK. The overall light blue color was camouflage to render the aircraft less visible at high altitude. The yellow and black stripes were a personal marking. Note the bomb under the nose; the G.IV was tail heavy after the bombs were dropped.

KZ   G.V 947/16

Gotha G.V(LVG) 947/16 of *Bogohl* 3, March 1918 in typical night bomber camouflage for the period using dark-colored printed camouflage fabric. The crew was *Lt*. von Korff, *Lt*. von Zedlitz, and *Gefr*. Speyer. The initials of the last names of the two officers in the crew comprised the personal marking.

AEG G.IV serial G.567/18 of *Staffel* 27, *Bogohl* 8b, flew tactical night bombing missions in the summer of 1918. The *staffel* number is on the fin; number 7 is the tactical number within the *staffel*. The camouflage is one typical style AEG used; another is the hexagon style seen on the AEG N.I below.

A typical AEG N.I in typical AEG factory finish for night bombers. The national insignia are barely visible. The AEG N.I carried six 50kg bombs under the wings. Production was limited because both *Idflieg* and the aircrews preferred the AEG G.IV and other twin-engine bombers.

Right: The gunner of a Gotha G.Va demonstrates the Gotha tunnel that enabled him to fire downward through the fuselage. The protective screens on either side of the cockpit to keep the gunner out of the propeller arcs are clearly shown, as are the external control cables to the tail and the over-wing fuel tank. Dark, printed camouflage fabric covers the entire airframe other than the engine nacelles.

Above: The twin-engine AEG design was originally designed as a *Kampfflugzeug* (battleplane), basically an aerial cruiser, and was designated the AEG K.I. The battleplane concept was inadequate for air combat; the AEG twin was too slow to intercept enemy aircraft. Its true role was soon determined to be bombing, and its designation was changed to AEG G.I, the 'G' standing for '*Grossflugzeug*', literally 'large aircraft,' in this case havng the connotation of twin-engine bomber. AEG was first to deliver a G-type, soon followed by Gotha, then Rumpler, Friedrichshafen, and Albatros.
Below: An early AEG G.I. The K.I had a pilot and front gunner; the G.I added a rear gunner for defense against fighters. With no engine cowlings the mechanical details are clearly visible and accessible to mechanics.

AEG bombers used a consistent configuration and airframe with more powerful engines for a heavier bomb load.
Top: The AEG G.II used 150 hp Benz Bz.III engines. Its vertical tail surfaces differed from other AEG bombers.
Center: The AEG G.III used 220 hp Mercedes D.IV straight-eight engines.
Bottom: The AEG G.IV used 260 hp Mercedes D.IVa six-cylinder engines.

Above: Rumpler entered the twin-engine bomber business with the Rumpler G.I. Like its Gotha and Freidrichshafen contemporaries it had pusher engines. Nose wheels protected against nose-overs on soft fields. The G.I used 150 hp Benz Bz.III engines, but only four were built before production was moved to the more powerful G.II using the same airframe.

Above: The Rumpler G.II was based on the Rumpler G.I airframe, but used more powerful 220 hp Benz Bz.IV engines. Performance and bombload were improved, and 24 were built. The Rumpler G.II served on both the Western and Macedonian Fronts as a bomber. In Macedonia it was also used to escort C-types during day bombing raids.

Left: The Rumpler G.III was a new design. Its 260 hp Mercedes D.IVa engines were mounted in nacelles above the wing. Thirty G.III bombers were built. Rumpler started designing a G.IV but its engineering resources were stretched too thin designing fighters and reconnaissance airplanes, and Rumpler dropped out of bombers.

Rumpler G.II G.109/15 assigned to *Kagohl* 2, summer of 1916. The light finish is from the factory but the black circles were identification markings painted at the unit level.

Rumpler G.III G311/16 assigned to *Kasta* 9, summer of 1917. By now the camouflage applied at the factory had changed to dark colors to camouflage the aircraft on the ground. The black circles with white star were a unit marking.

Friedrichshafen G.IIIa 862/18 of *Bogohl* 8 in flight, October 1918. This aircraft has dark printed camouflage fabric for its role as a night bomber. The revised 'box tail' with two rudders and biplane horizontal tail surfaces gave better controllability with an engine out and distinguishes the G.IIIa from the earlier G.III with single vertical fin and rudder and monoplane tail. The object on the nose is a parachute; the aircraft was employed for parachute testing on this flight.

Top: The Friedrichshafen G.III used 260 hp Mercedes D.IVa engines mounted in nacelles above the wing.
Right: The Albatros G.II prototype powered by 150 hp Benz engines.
Bottom: About two dozen Albatros G.III bombers were built. Using 220 hp Benz Bz.IV engines, it eliminated the G.II's nose wheels to reduce weight and drag. Its thick wing differs from most Albatros designs.

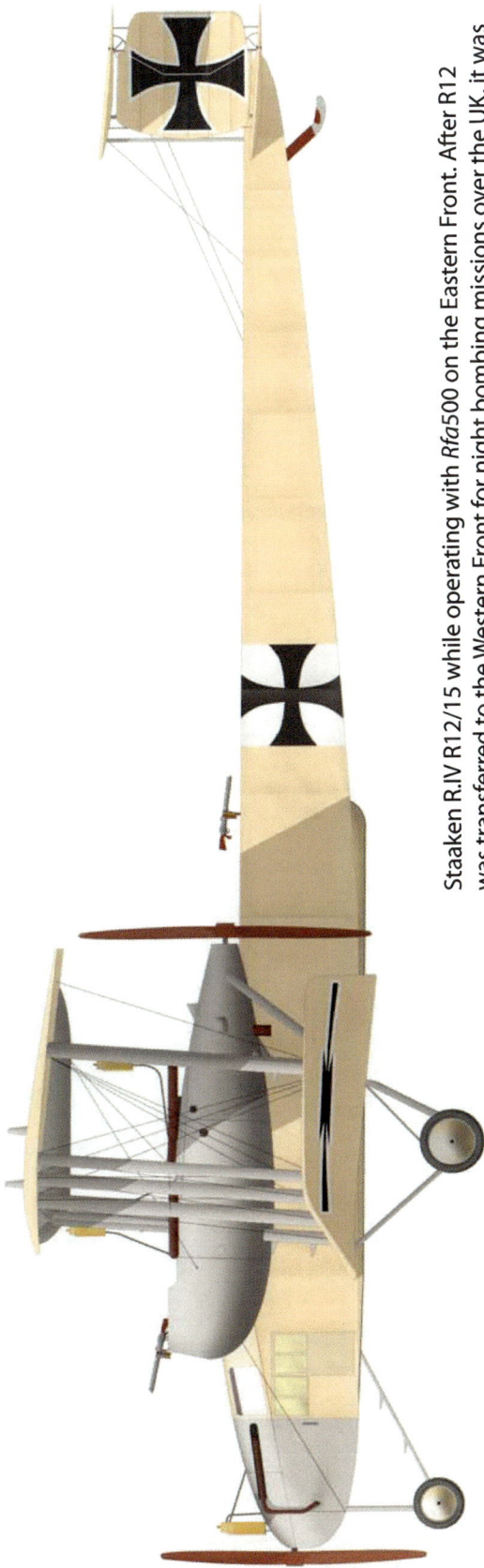

Staaken R.IV R12/15 while operating with *Rfa500* on the Eastern Front. After R12 was transferred to the Western Front for night bombing missions over the UK, it was camouflaged in dark colors similar to the R.VI adjacent. Only one R.IV was built but it was very successful, and was the only R-plane to serve on both fronts. Six engines coupled in pairs drove three propellers.

Staaken R.VI R27/16 was camouflaged in dark night colors for night bombing missions over the UK. Interestingly, the engine nacelles on this aircraft were left in natural metal rather than being painted a dark color as was more common. The camouflage was apparently applied at the factory because the national insignia are white outlines applied over the camouflage. The R.VI was the main production R-plane, with 18 being built by Staaken and three other manufacturers. Most were powered by four 260 hp Mercedes D.IVa engines, but some used the 245 hp Maybach Mb.IVa. Armament was 4–6 machine guns. Span was 42.2 meters (138.5 feet).

Bombers Large and Small (R, N, GL, & L Types)

Several other categories remain to be discussed. Earliest are the **R-types**, standing for *Reisenflugzeug*, or giant aircraft. These were huge, multi-engine, long-range bombers primarily for night bombing. In this context 'multi-engine' meant more than two engines, and R-planes with three to six engines were flown on operations. The German army was interested in the R-plane as an alternative to the costly Zeppelin, and in late 1916 the army gave up on the vulnerable airships and offered its remaining airships to the German navy. The navy was interested in R-planes to supplement Zeppelins for long-range reconnaissance for the fleet, and ordered R-planes to both floatplane and flying boat configurations.

Given the inability to feather the fixed-pitch wood propellers of the time, a major challenge was how to avoid the immense drag of a wind-milling propeller in event of engine failure. This lead to many R-planes being designed with centralized power systems that connected the engines to gearboxes via clutches and drove the propellers via extension shafts. This was complex and heavy, and R-planes with separate engines and propellers were more successful on operations. To counter problems with engine failure, one requirement was that mechanics have access to repair the engines in flight.

At the other end of the spectrum were the single-engine night bombers, or **N-types**, discussed above. Initially standard C-types were used for tactical night bombing, but *Idflieg* wanted a two-seater specifically designed for night bombing that could carry a heavier bomb load. Although a number of prototypes were built, the AEG C.IVn, (the 'n' suffix for *nacht* – night), an extended-span development of the AEG C.IV, was the first (and main) production type. Early in its production run *Idflieg* promulgated the 'N' category for single-engine night bombers

Left: The rare AEG N.I was an extended-span development of the AEG C.IV; the truss bracing the forward upper wing spar is clearly visible. Many wore the standard AEG night-bomber camouflage shown here. Few N-types were built; larger G-types were preferred for night bombing.

Below: The huge Staaken R.VI was the most widely-produced giant aircraft and was used to bomb Britain by night; R.28 is shown here. Four 260 hp Mercedes D.IVa engines, each driving its own propeller, powered most R.VI aircraft.

Above: The massive SSW R.VIII displays its 48 m (157' 6") wingspan; it was the largest aircraft built by any nation during the war, but never flew. It was powered by six 300 hp Basse & Selve BuS.IVa engines in the fuselage geared together to drive the propellers and allowing a failed engine to be de-coupled from the gearbox via a clutch. This complex, heavy arrangement was needed to avoid the drag of a wind-milling propeller in event of an engine failure.

and the remaining aircraft were designated AEG N.I. These were used in small numbers but German preference was to use G-types for this task, limiting the number of N-types built.

Finally, late in the war two more categories were created. The **L-type** (three-engine) was intermediate between the two-engine G-type and multi-engine R-type. The **GL-type**, or light (*licht*) G-type, was a smaller, faster twin-engine bomber and long-range photo-reconnaissance category. However, no GL or L-type achieved general production or operational service during the war.

Above: The VGO.I was the ancestor of the Staaken R-planes, which continued its basic wing and fuselage design through many engine configurations.

Right: The Gotha GL.VII was an attempt to produce a fast day bomber and long-range reconnaissance plane. Many variations of the basic configuration were tested.

Above & Below: Nose details of a Gotha GL.IX. The front gunner position was eliminated to save weight and drag, the bomber depending on speed and its rear gunner for protection. Put into limited production, the GL.IX was too late to reach operational units before the armistice. Twenty were delivered to Belgium after the war, where this one was photographed. Development of this series of designs was prolonged due to the difficulty of achieving the desired high-altitude speed, climb, and ceiling.

Above: The AEG G.IVk was an anti-tank airplane. Engine nacelles and the cockpit area were armored. Gunners fore and aft each had downward-firing 20mm Becker cannon for destroying tanks and a flexible machine gun to defend against enemy fighters. Five of these were delivered to the front before the armistice, but it is not known if they were used in combat. 260 hp Mercedes D.IVa engines.

Above: The AEG G.V was developed from the G.IV by extending the wingspan for greater bombload. Servo-tabs on the ailerons helped the pilot by reducing control forces. Power was the reliable 260 hp Mercedes D.IVa.

Right: Despite having a 'G' designation, the Roland G.I was powered by only one 240 hp Maybach Mb.IV engine driving two propellers via gears and shafts. Only one was built.

Force Composition

In addition to the difference in procurement policies between Germany and the Allies, it is also interesting to examine the composition of their air services by type of aircraft. The table below shows this composition in August 1918. Germany had nearly the same number of fighters and reconnaissance airplanes, with a small number of bombers. This reflected the value of reconnaissance, the most important function of WW1 aviation, and her defensive stance.

The United States Air Service had a very similar composition, as did Italy. France had a larger number of bombers, reflecting a more offensive mode of operations. Great Britain deviated most, with a larger proportion of fighters and bombers, reflecting her more offensive operations. In particular, Great Britain used fighters extensively for ground attack.

Composition of Allied and Central Powers Air Forces by Type in August 1918

Air Service	Fighter	Observation	Bomber
France	34%	51%	15%
Great Britain	55%	23%	22%
Italy	46%	45%	9%
United States	46.5%	46.5%	7%
Germany	42%	50%	8%
Austria-Hungary	63%	28%	9%

Aviation Casualties

The table below lists aviation casualties for the main antagonists on the Western Front. The large number of British casualties compared to the other countries was a result of the constant British offensive air operations. By comparison, both France and Germany were more conservative in their air operations to limit causalties. The light American casualties reflect the limited time the USAS was engaged over the Western Front. Painful as these numbers are, they are small compared to the terrible casualties amongst the infantry.

WWI Aviation Casualties

	British	French	American	Total Allied	German
Killed	6,166	2,872	681	9,719	5,853
Wounded	7,245	2,922	127	10,294	7,302
Missing	3,212	1,461	72	4,745	2,751
Total	**16,623**	**7,255**	**880**	**23,758**	**15,906**

Below: This Fokker D.VII without its fabric covering shows its simple welded steel tube fuselage and innovative plywood wing structure. The wing was key to its success, offering exceptional maneuverabilty and handling qualities and great strength while enabling elimination of drag-producing bracing wires.

Frontbeststand Inventory of All Classes of Army Aircraft at the Front

Class Total and Percent of Grand Total	1914			1915						1916						1917						1918			
	31 Aug	31 Oct	31 Dec	28 Feb	30 Apr	30 Jun	31 Aug	31 Oct	31 Dec	28 Feb	30 Apr	30 Jun	31 Aug	31 Oct	31 Dec	28 Feb	30 Apr	30 Jun	31 Aug	31 Oct	31 Dec	28 Feb	30 Apr	30 Jun	31 Aug
A Class Total	44	36	53	65	56	37	13	16	13	10	7	2													
Percent of Total	*20.2*	*14.3*	*15.4*	*14.4*	*8.7*	*5.0*	*1.6*	*1.5*	*1.1*	*0.8*	*0.5*	*0.1*													
B Class Total	173	209	283	379	581	589	580	597	396	198	176	60	13	22	21	9	9	7	5	4	4	4	4	7	9
Percent of Total	*79.3*	*83.3*	*82.5*	*84.2*	*90.2*	*79.6*	*70.7*	*58.3*	*33.1*	*15.2*	*12.1*	*4.1*	*0.9*	*1.2*	*1.0*	*0.4*	*0.4*	*0.2*	*0.1*	*0.1*	*0.1*	*0.1*	*0.1*	*0.2*	*0.2*
C Class Total			4		2	91	181	318	660	934	1029	1184	1302	1487	1508	1561	1557	1966	2061	1821	1797	1475	1611	1528	1610
Percent of Total			*1.2*		*0.3*	*12.3*	*22.1*	*31.0*	*55.2*	*71.8*	*71.0*	*81.2*	*85.1*	*79.1*	*71.9*	*72.0*	*67.0*	*66.8*	*64.2*	*56.6*	*44.2*	*36.1*	*33.7*	*34.9*	*34.5*
CL Class Total																					332	519	751	609	604
Percent of Total																					*8.1*	*12.7*	*15.7*	*13.9*	*13.0*
Lichtbildflug. Class Total																				11	64	51	95	82	177
Percent Total																				*0.3*	*1.6*	*1.2*	*2.0*	*1.9*	*3.8*
D Class Total										1		8	62	265	485	562	686	875	1030	1224	1566	1592	1769	1614	1691
Percent of Total										*0.1*		*0.5*	*4.1*	*14.1*	*23.1*	*25.9*	*29.5*	*29.8*	*32.1*	*38.1*	*38.5*	*38.9*	*37.1*	*36.9*	*36.3*
Dr Class Total																			2	17	35	143	180	125	66
Percent of Total																			*0.1*	*0.5*	*0.9*	*3.5*	*3.8*	*2.9*	*1.4*
E Class Total			2			4	22	58	107	142	229	191	124	57	17	3	2	1		10	7				80
Percent of Total			*0.6*			*0.5*	*2.7*	*5.7*	*8.9*	*10.9*	*15.8*	*13.1*	*8.1*	*3.0*	*0.8*	*0.1*	*0.1*	*0.1*		*0.3*	*0.2*				*1.7*
G Class Total						2	6	20	20	13	7	13	28	48	46	34	71	86	111	116	155	156	206	216	223
Percent of Total						*0.3*	*0.7*	*2.0*	*1.7*	*1.0*	*0.5*	*1.0*	*1.8*	*2.6*	*2.2*	*1.6*	*3.0*	*2.9*	*3.4*	*3.6*	*3.8*	*3.8*	*4.3*	*4.9*	*4.8*
J Class Total																		7	2	12	76	113	139	184	186
Percent of Total																		*0.2*	*0.1*	*0.4*	*1.9*	*2.8*	*2.9*	*4.2*	*4.0*
N Class Total																				2	31	37	19	9	13
Percent of Total																				*0.1*	*0.8*	*0.9*	*0.4*	*0.2*	*0.3*
Miscellaneous Total	1	6	1	6	5	17	18	15		2	1														
Percent of Total	*0.5*	*2.4*	*0.3*	*1.3*	*0.9*	*2.3*	*2.2*	*1.5*		*0.2*	*0.1*														
Grand Total:	218	251	343	450	644	740	820	1024	1196	1300	1449	1458	1529	1879	2097	2169	2325	2942	3211	3217	4067	4090	4774	4374	4659

Above: The Junkers J.I was very effective in combat and was highly popular with its crews due to its resistance to ground fire. Its production was limited by its complex all-metal structure that required specialized techniques and tools. The metal alloy used for the structure was also in short supply. At the end of the war Germany led the Allies in aerodynamics and structures, while the Allies led in powerful V-8 and V-12 engines.

German Naval Aircraft

Germany was predominately a land power and depended on her Army to win the war on the Western Front. Consequently, the lion's share of aviation resources went to the *Luftstreitkräfte* and German naval aviation was a distant second priority for resource allocation; only about 5% of German aircraft (about 2,365) were built for the Navy.

Due to the immature state of airplane development, the German navy relied on Zeppelins for fleet reconnaissance due to their great range and endurance. Airplanes were initially limited to short-range reconnaissance from naval air stations. However, as airplane technology advanced, torpedo planes were developed for offensive anti-ship operations, and floatplane fighters were developed to defend the naval air stations.

Aerial torpedo operations quickly showed the slow torpedo planes were too vulnerable to anti-aircraft fire, and most were reassigned to bombing and long-range reconnaissance missions.

British anti-submarine operations over the North Sea spurred development of longer-range two-seat floatplane fighters to combat the British flying boats. Combats between the German floatplanes and British flying boats were frequent and intense in 1917 and 1918.

The navy was also interested in long-range 'giant' seaplanes for reconnaissance to supplement the costly, vulnerable Zeppelins, and several types were built.

Growth of Naval Aviation During the War

Country/Dates	Airplanes	Airships	Balloons	Men
Austria-Hungary				
28 July 1914	22	—	—	—
4 November 1918	249	—	—	—
France				
4 August 1914	8	—	—	208
11 November 1918	1,264	37	198	11,059
Germany				
1 August 1914	24	1	—	~200
11 November 1918	1,478	19	—	16,122
Great Britain				
4 August 1914	93	6	~2	727
1 April 1918	2,949	111	~200	55,066
Italy				
23 May 1915	15	3	2	385
4 November 1918	638	36	16	4,382
Russia				
1 August 1914	24	0	?	?
30 June 1917	~200	0	?	?
United States				
6 April 1917	54	1	2	267
11 November 1918	2,107	20	117	39,871

Note 1: First dates given for each country are the dates they declared war.

Note 2: Last date for Great Britain is the date the RAF was formed and the RNAS dis-established.

Below: A Friedrichshafen FF33 is recovered by a warship after a mission. Most FF33 series used the 150 hp Benz Bz.III engine.

Kriegsschiff nimmt Seeflugzeug an Deck.

Above: The Friedrichshafen FF33 series was the most common observation floatplane; here FF33E #738 rendezvouses with a U-boat. The FF33 was noted for its robust construction and good sea keeping.
Below: The Friedrichshafen FF49c replaced the FF33 in production. The more powerful 200 hp Benz Bz.IV engine was fitted to carry more more fuel for longer endurance.

Left: The little-known Sablatnig SF2 was built in small numbers to supplement the Friedrichshafen FF33 and FF49c reconnaissance floatplanes. It was powered by the 160 hp Mercedes D.III. The similar SF5 succeeded it in production and service.

Left: The Sablatnig SF5 was developed from the SF2 and replaced it in production. Instead of the Mercedes, the SF5 used the 150 hp Benz Bz.III, freeing Mercedes production for fighters. The Sablatnigs were not as robust as the Friedrichshafens and did not have as good sea-keeping. Nor did they offer the exceptional performance and maneuverability of the Brandenburg W12 and its successors.

Right: Sablatnig SF5 seaplanes in operation at Libau.

Above: The Brandenburg GW was a typical German floatplane torpedo bomber design. It was powered by a pair of 160 hp Mercedes D.III engines.

Above: Like the other designs, the Brandenburg GW had trouble lifting a torpedo, plus torpedo operations proved to be highly succeptiable to anti-aircraft fire. Torpedo operations were eventually abandoned and most of the torpedo bombers were reassigned to long-range reconnaissance duties.
Left: The Friedrichshafen FF41a was powered by a pair of 150 hp Benz Bz.III engines. Marine #1000 sank a grounded Russian destroyer by bombing in the Gulf of Riga.
Below: The Gotha WD 14 was powered by a pair of 200 hp Benz Bz.IV engines. For long-range reconnaissance duties jettisonable fuel tanks were carried in the torpedo slings.

Above: When the German Navy requested single-seat floatplane fighters, Albatros responded with their W4, which was based on their D.I fighter and used the same fuselage, fin, and 160 hp Mercedes D.III engine. The W4 had larger wings to support the extra weight of the floats and a larger tail to balance them. The first production batch had one machine gun, but subsequent batches had two guns. The W4 tied for best German single-seat floatplane fighter with the Rumpler 6B1.
Below: The KDW was Brandenburg's response to the single-seat floatplane fighter requirement. Based on their KD fighter, used as the Brandenburg D.I by the Austro-Hungarians but not by Germany, the KDW had larger wings to support the additional weight of its floats plus one synchronized gun. Marine #748 shown here was the prototype, yet downed a Sikorski Ilya Mouromets in Septermber 1916, one of only three downed by German aircraft during the war.

Above: Rumpler's response to the single-seat floatplane fighter requirement was their 6B1 derived from their C.I two-seat reconnaissance airplane. Elimination of the observer and his gun compensated for the additional weight of the floats, and the 6B1 used the same wings as the C.I although the upper wing was moved forward to compensate for the elimination of the observer's weight aft and the forard weight of the floats. Surprisingly, the 6B1 was as successful on operations as the Albatros W4 and more successful than the KDW. The 6B1 had much better flying qualities than the faster KDW.

Below: Rumpler developed the 6B1 into the 6B2, which eliminated the propeller spinner based on Rumpler's development of their C.IV reconnaissance plane. Designed to carry two guns instead of the one fitted to the 6B1, about half the production aircraft had only one gun. Both the 6B1 and 6B2 used the 160 hp Mercedes D.III engine. The 6B2 saw limited service due to the tremendous success of the Brandenburg W12 two-seat floatplane fighter.

Left: Roland developed their single-seat W fighter from their C.II two-seater. Only one prototype was built. It was powered by the popular 160 hp Mercedes D.III engine.

Left: Friedrichshafen's response to the request for a single-seat fighter floatplane with the neat, streamlined FF43 using the 160 hp Mercedes D.III engine. Despite its sleek appearance, only one prototype was built.

Below: The innovative Ursinus fighter featured retractable floats, a very advanced feature for the time that unfortunately had too many mechanical problems.

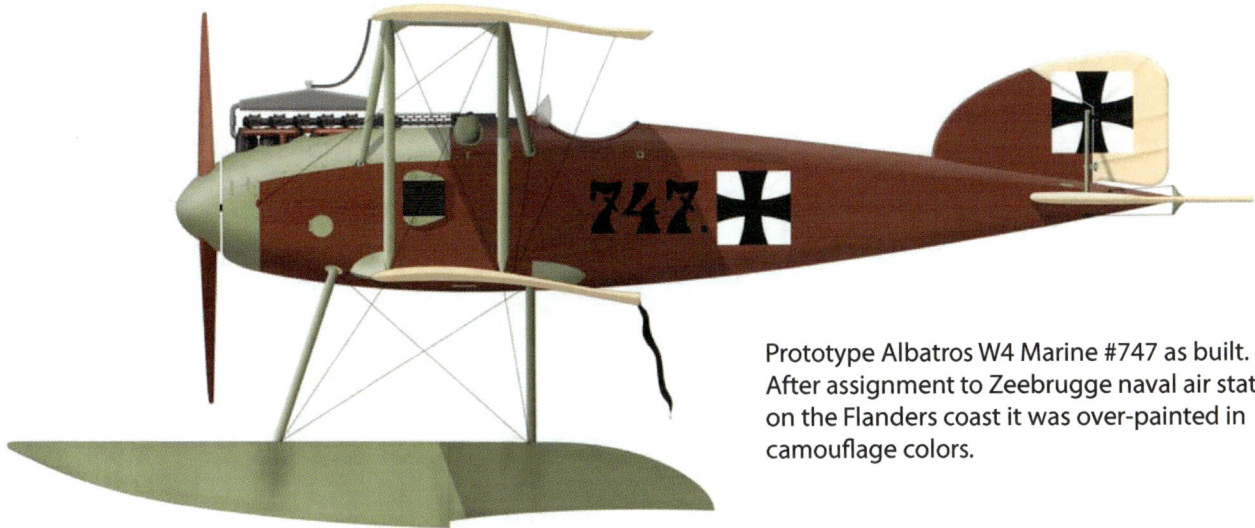

Prototype Albatros W4 Marine #747 as built. After assignment to Zeebrugge naval air station on the Flanders coast it was over-painted in camouflage colors.

Prototype Rumpler 6B1 Marine #751 after being re-painted upon assignment to Zeebrugge naval air station on the Flanders coast. *Lt.z.s.* Neimeyer used Rumpler 6B1 #751 to down a Short Seaplane on 31 Aug. 1916 and a Caudron G.4 on 7 Sept. 1916.

Prototype Brandenburg CC Marine #946 in plain finish as built. Germany had no love for flying boats in the cold waters in the North Sea and Baltic and the CC was used only briefly; it was much more successful in Austro-Hungarian service in the warmer Adriatic.

Above: The KDW was subject to a continuing series of modifications to improve its tricky handling characteristics. This late-production model features two guns in front of the pilot and outboard bracing struts to stiffen the upper wing for improved aileron response. Power was a 150–160 hp Benz, Mercedes, or Maybach.

Above Right: The Brandenburg W25 was yet another attempt to improve the KDW by replacing the heavy star-struts with conventional wing bracing and installing ailerons on all four wings. It was not considered for production due to the great success of the two-seat Brandenburg W12. Power was a 150 hp Benz Bz.III.

Right: With its floats retracted the Ursinus fighter was very streamlined for its day. Power was a 150 hp Benz Bz.III.

Above & Below: Disappointed with the operational limitations of its single-seat floatplane fighters, which could intercept opposing reconnaissance airplanes but could not undertake offensive operations or compete with land-based fighters, the German Navy requested two-seat floatplane fighters. The innovative Brandenburg W12 was a breakthrough two-seat floatplane fighter design. Its clever integration of float bracing struts nearly eliminated the need for drag-producing bracing wires. More important, the W12 had the speed and maneuverability of the similarly-powered single-seat floatplanes coupled with the great advantage of a gunner with flexible gun. The gunner also helped with over-water navigation and operated the wireless if fitted; single-seaters did not carry wireless. The W12 and its successors fought very effectively over the North Sea against British flying boats on anti-submarine operations and made such an impact that it inspired all subsequent German floatplane fighter designs. W12 Marine #2008 below has just made an emergency landing and the four-leaf clover must have worked; the aircraft and crew are undamaged.

Above: Using the 240–260 hp Maybach Mb.IVa, the Brandenburg W19 was an enlarged, more powerful derivative of the W12 for longer range and greater payload. Its excellent design and additional power gave it nearly the same speed and maneuverability as the smaller W12.

Right: A formation of Brandenburg fighters, two W29s and a W19, on patrol over the North Sea.

Below: The Brandenburg W29 was developed from the W12 for greater speed. Using the same basic 150–160 hp engines used by the W12, its monoplane design reduced drag and significantly increased its speed, which was very useful to intercept the large British flying boats patrolling over the North Sea on anti-submarine operations.

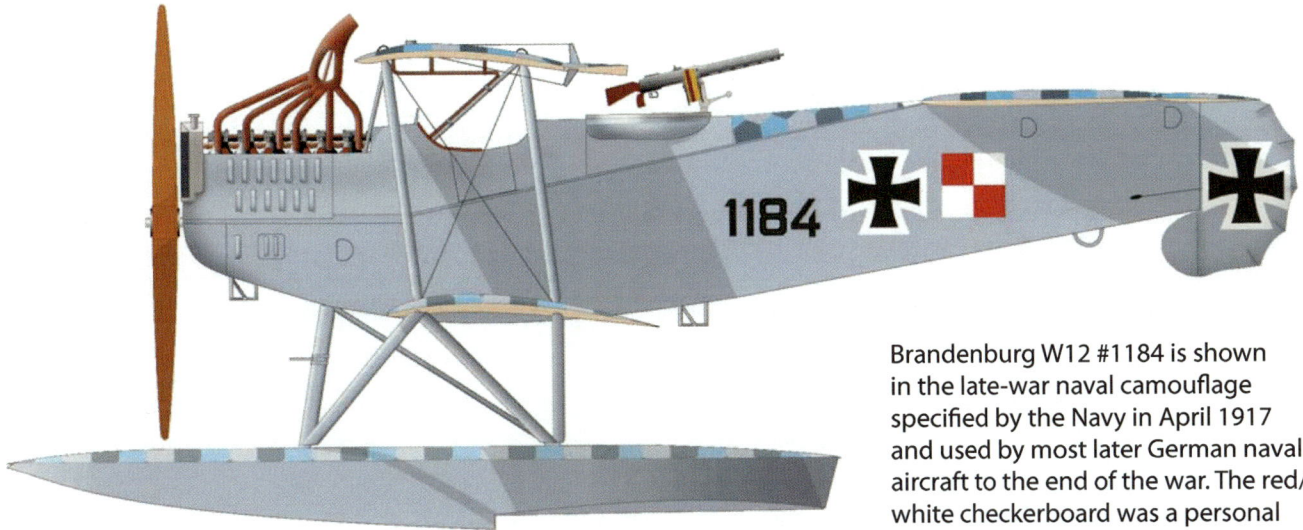

Brandenburg W12 #1184 is shown in the late-war naval camouflage specified by the Navy in April 1917 and used by most later German naval aircraft to the end of the war. The red/white checkerboard was a personal marking. This aircraft served at Zeebrugge Naval Air Station.

This W29 was the personal aircraft of *Oblt.z.S.* Friedrich Christiansen and was used by him to lead the attack that disabled British submarine *C25* on July 6, 1918. The black initial 'C' for 'Christiansen' in a black diamond painted over a white stripe on the rear fuselage was Christiansen's personal insignia.

Brandenburg W29 Marine #2532 displays the standard naval camouflage with the two white fuselage stripes indicating assignment to Norderney Naval Air Station.

Above: The Albatros W8 was an unsuccessful competitor to the Brandenburg W12. Power was the experimental 195 hp Benz Bz.IIIb V-8.

Right: The Friedrichshafen FF63 powered by the 200 hp Benz Bz.IV was an unsuccessful competitor to the Brandenburg monoplanes.

Left: Brandenburg enlarged the W12 into the W19 for longer range and more payload, and created the monoplane W29 for more speed. The logical next step was an enlarged monoplane to combine greater speed and greater range, and that was done in the W33. Speed and maneuverability were comparable to the smaller W29 due to its greater power.

Right: The Brandenburg CC was a successful flying boat fighter, but German crews preferred floatplanes in the chill waters they operated in and the CC did not long remain in German service. In the warmer waters of the Adriatic it was a great success operating with the Austro-Hungarian Navy. The CC used the star-struts of the KDW; this prototype mounts one machine gun. Power for the German CC was the 150 hp Benz Bz.III.

Right: Powered by the 230 hp Hiero, the Brandenburg W18 was a more powerful derivative of the CC. Fitted with two guns, only one was supplied to the German Navy but it was a great success operating with the Austro-Hungarian Navy. The CC used the star-struts of the KDW, but the W18 used conventional interplane struts, which weighed less and made the wings stiffer in torsion for better aileron response.

Below: The diminutive Brandenburg W20 was designed to operate from submarines; three prototypes were built.

Navy Landplanes S & LF Numbers

Reference TA 239E T1022 R1057

S #	Type	W/N	Engine	Class	S #	Type	W/N	Engine	Class
1	Alb.				47	Alb. DD	462	D.I	FT
2	Alb. B./13				48	Alb. DD	474	D.I	
3	Alb. B.I				49	Alb. DD	479	D.I	
4	Alb.				50	Alb. DD	517	D.I	
5	Alb.				51	Alb. DD	519	D.I	
6	Ago				52	Caspar?			
7	Ago				53	Alb. B.I	395	Bz.III	
8	Ru. Taube				54	Alb. B.I	396	Bz.III	
9	Ru. Taube	183	As.I		55	Alb. B.I	394	Bz.III	
10	Bleriot				56	Ago DD	140	100 Gn	
11	Alb.			FT	57	Ago DD	80	100 Gn	
12	Alb.				58	Ago DD	125	100 Gn	
13	Alb. B.II		D.I		59	Ru. DD	264	Merc	
14	Alb. B.II		85 Merc		60	Ru. B.I	250	D.I	
15	Ago				61	Ru. B.I	262	D.I	
16	Ago			Pusher	62	Ru. B.I	265	D.I	
17	Ago			Monoplane	63	Ru. B.I	261	D.I	
18	Rathjen				64	Ru. B.I	263		
19	Ru.				65	Ru. DD	448		
20	Ru. Taube				66	Ago C.II	128	Bz.III	MG
21	Ru. Taube				67	Ago C.II	129	Bz.III	MG
22	Ru. Taube		100		68	Alb.		100	
23	Ago				69	Alb.			
24	Alb.		D.I		70	Fok. E.I		U.0	MG
24	Fok. M7	101	U.0		71	Fok.			
25	Ago				72	Fok. E.III		U.I	MG
25	Fok. M5L	105	U.0		73	Fok. E.III		U.I	MG
26	Ago				74	Fok. E.IIIF.2 II MFA		U.I	MG
26	Fok. M5L	104	U.0		75	Alb.			
27	Ago				76	Alb. B.II	572	D.I	
27	Fok. M5L	105	U.0		77	Alb. B.II		D.I	
28	Schwade I		100 Stak *illegible original		78	Alb. B	494	D.I	
29	Alb. B.I	375	D.I		79	Alb. B.II			
30	Alb. B.I		D.I		80	Alb. DD	475	D.I	
31	Alb. DD	374	D.I		81	Alb. Schül DD	500	85 Bz	
32	DFW DD	87	Bz.III		82	Alb. Schül DD	504	85 Bz	
33	Alb.				83	Alb. DD	416	Rp.III	
34	Alb. B.II		D.I		84	Alb. C	987	Rp.III	MG
35	AEG				85	Alb. C		Rp.III	MG, B
35	Aviatik		200		86	Alb. C.I		Rp.III	MG, B
36	Ago DD	81	100 Gn		87	Alb. DD	1040	Rp.III	MG, B
37	Ru DD	236	Bz.III		88	Alb. DD	1041	Rp.III	MG, B
38	Ru DD	238	Bz.III		89	Alb. DD	1065	Rp.III	MG, B
39	Ru DD		Bz.III		90	Alb. C.I	1066	Rp.III	MG, B
40	Ru DD				91	Alb. DD		Rp.III	
41	Ru DD	237	Bz.III		92	Alb. DD		Rp.III	MG
42	Ru. Taube	170	D.I	ex. A.131/13	93	Ru. DD	287	D.I	
43	Ru. Taube	172	D.I	ex. A.133/13	94	Ru. DD	288	D.I	
44	Alb. DD	457	D.I		95	Ru. DD	289	D.I	
45	Alb. DD	463	D.I	FT	96	Bleriot			
46	Alb. DD	461	D.I		97	LVG	538	D.I	

S #	Type	W/N	Engine	Class	S #	Type	W/N	Engine	Class
98	LVG	539	D.I		152	Alb. DD	811	Bz.III	
99	LVG B.II		D.I		153	Alb. B.I	421	D.I	
100	LVG B.II		D.I		154	Alb. B.I	422	D.I	
101	LVG B.II		D.I		155	Alb. B.I	423	D.I	
102	LVG		D.I		156	Alb. DD B.1016/14	448	D.I	ex.
103	LVG B.II		D.I		157	Alb. B.1017/14	449	D.I	ex.
104	LVG B.II	546	D.I		158	Ago C.I	364	Bz.III	MG
105	LVG B.II	547	D.I		159	Ago C.I	367	Bz.III	
106	LVG B.II	548	D.I		160	Ago C.I	368	Bz.III	MG
107					161	Ago C.I	407	D.III	
108	Brand.	WD3	D.III		162	Ago C.I		D.III	MG, B
109	LVG DD	629	100		163	Ru. B.I	457	D.I	
110	LVG C.I		Bz.III		164	AEG C		Bz.III	MG, B
111	Alb. B.I	473	D.I		165	Brand DD	51	Bz.III	MG, B
112	Alb. DD	666	D.I		166	Brand		Bz.III	MG, B
113	Alb. B.II			MG	167	Brand DD		Bz.III	2MG, B
114	Alb. B.II		D.I		168	Brand		Bz.III	MG, B
115	Alb. DD	668	D.I		169	Brand		Bz.III	MG, B
116	Alb.				170	Brand		Bz.III	MG, B
117	Alb.		D.I		171	Alb. B.III	902	D.I	B
118	Alb. DD	685			172	Alb. B.III	932	D.I	B
119	Alb. DD	685	D.I	FT	173	Alb. DD	938	D.I	B
120	Alb. B.II	694	D.I		174	Alb. DD	897	D.I	B
121	Alb. B.II	731	D.I		175				
122	Alb. B.II	732	D.I		176	Alb. DD	1134	D.I	B, FT
123	Alb. B.II	756	D.I		177			Bz.III	MG, B
124	Alb. DD	757	D.I		178	Fok. E.III		U.I	MG
125	Alb. C.I		Bz.III	2MG	179	Fok. E.III		U.I	MG
126	Alb. C.I		Bz.III	2MG	180	Ago C.I		D.III	MG, FT, B
127	Alb. C.I		Bz.III	MG	181	Ago C.I		D.III	MG, FT, B
128	Ru. DD	275	Rp.III		182	Ago C.I		D.III	MG, FT, B
129	Ru. B.I		Rp.III		183	Ago C.I		D.III	MG, FT, B
130	Ru.		150		184	Ago C.I		D.III	MG, B
131	Ru.		150		185	Ago C.I		D.III	MG
132	Ru.		150		186	Fok. E.III		U.I	MG
133	Ru. DD	449	Bz.III		187	Fok. E.III			MG
134	Ru. B.I	450	Bz.III		188	Fok. E.III		U.I	MG
135	Ru. DD	318	As.I		189				MG
136	Rathgen DD	6	As.I		190	Fok. E.III		U.I	MG
137	Rathgen DD	7	As.I		191	Fok. E.I		U.0	MG
138	Alb.	539	100		192	Fok. E.I		U.0	MG
139	Bleriot				193	Fok. E.I		U.0	MG
140	Alb. DD	799	Bz.III		194	Fok. E.I		U.0	MG
141	Alb. DD	807	Bz.III		195	Fok. E.I		U.0	MG
142	Alb. DD	808	Bz.III	MG	196	Fok. E.III	480	U.I	MG
143	Alb. C.I		Bz.III	MG FT, B	197	Rathjen		100	
144	Alb. C.I	993	Bz.III	2MG, B	198	Rathjen		100	
145	Alb.		D.III	MG	199	Alb. B.III			
146	Alb. C		D.III	MG	200	Alb. C.III		D.III	2MG, FT
147	Alb. C.I	1163			201	Alb. C		D.III	2MG, FT
148	Alb. C		D.III	MG, FT	202	Alb. C		D.III	2MG, FT
149	Alb. C		D.III	MG, FT	203	Alb. C		D.III	2MG, FT
150	Alb. DD	805	Bz.III	MG					
151	Alb. C.I	809	Bz.III	MG, B					

S #	Type	W/N	Engine	Class	S #	Type	W/N	Engine	Class
204				2MG, FT	230	Fok. E.III		U.I	MG
205				2MG, FT	231	Fok. E.III		U.I	MG
206	Alb. C.III			2MG, FT	232	Alb. C		Bz.III	2MG
207	Alb. C		Bz.III	MG, FT	233	Alb. C		Bz.III	2MG
208	Fok. E.I		U.0	MG	234	Alb. C		Bz.III	2MG
209			150 hp	MG, FT	235	Alb. C.III		Bz.III	2MG
210	Fok. E.IV	568	U.III	2MG	236	Fok. D.II		U.I	
211	Fok. E.III		U.I	MG	237	Fok. D.II		U.I	
212	Fok. E.III		U.I	MG	238	Fok. D.II	803	U.0	
213	Alb. C.III		Bz.III	MG, FT	239	AEG		D.III	
214	Alb.		Bz.III	MG	240	AEG		D.III	
215	Fok. D.I		D.I	MG	241	Fok. D.II		U.I	
216	Fok. D.I		D.I	MG	242	Fok. D.II		U.I	
217	Fok. D.I		D.I	MG	243	Hannuschke		100	
218	Fok. D.I		D.I	MG	244	Bristol			
219	Fok. D.I		D.I	MG	245				
220	Fok. D.I		D.I	MG	246			U.0	
221	Fok. E.III		U.I	MG	247			U.0	
222	Fok. E.III		U.I	MG	248				
223	Pfal. E.V		D.I	MG	249				
224	Pfal. E.V		D.I	MG	250				
225	Fok. E.III		U.I	MG					
226	Fok. E.III		U.I	MG	—	Bleriot			
227	Alb. C		Bz.III	2MG					
228	Alb. C		Bz.III	2MG	300	Ru. 4A15		2x	
229	Alb. C		Bz.III	MG, FT	301	RML 1		3xMbHS	

Above: This Fokker D.II is Navy Landplane serial LF238 (LF = *landflugzeug*), Fokker works number 803. The Fokker D.II was powered by a 100 hp Oberursel U.I 9-cylinder rotary and carried one synchronized gun.

Above: Throughout the war the German Navy relied on Zeppelins for long-range reconnaissance for their High Seas Fleet. The Zeppelins were fragile and costly to build and maintain, and as airplanes improved in performance, the Navy began to consider using Giant seaplanes for this task. Prof. Dornier at the Zeppelin-Lindau factory designed several all-metal Giant flying boats for this requirement. Above, the Dornier Rs.III taxiis for take-off. The Dornier Rs.III was the only giant seaplane to see operational service with the German Navy.

Below: The Dornier Rs.IV was the next all-metal flying boat, seen here under test, was too late to reach operational service with the German Navy and after the armistice was converted to a passenger seaplane.

German Seaplane Numbers

Mr. #	Type	Class	Engine	Mr. #	Type	Class	Engine
E1	Rumpler Taube		100 Argus	70	Ago		As.III
D2	Albatros		70 Merc.	71	Ago		As.III
D3	Albatros WMZ			72	Ago		U.III
E4	Rumpler Taube		100 Argus	71–72	Brandenburg W		Mb.III
D5	Albatros WMZ		75 Nag		*Numbers 71–72 re-assigned to Brandenburg trainers*		
D6	Curtis			73	Union		120 AD
D7	Ago		100 Argus	74	Albatros		Bz.III
E8	Rumpler Taube		100 Argus	75	Oertz FB2		As.II
D9	Albatros WMZ		As.I	76–85	FF19	B	D.I
D10	Albatros WMZ		As.I	86–90	Rumpler 4B11		D.I
D11	Albatros WMZ		As.I	91–98	FF29A	B	D.I
D12	Avro		100 Gnome	99–100	FF33A	B	D.I
13	Wight		Salmson	101–110	Rumpler 4B12	B	Bz.III
14	Albatros		D.I	111	Albatros		D.I
D15	Ago		145 Argus	112	Ago		100 Ob
D16	Albatros		As.II	113	Ago		100 Ob
D17	Albatros WMZ		Bz.I	114	Ago		100 Ob
D18	Curtis		90 Curtiss	115	Ago C.Iw	CB	Bz.III
D19	Ago		100 Gnome	116	Lohner (Br.AE)		Bz.III
20	Albatros	FT	D.I	117	FF34	CHFT	Mb.IV
21	Albatros		D.I	118	Gotha WD5		D.III
22	Albatros		D.I	119	Gotha WD7		2xD.II
23	Albatros		As.II	120	Gotha UWD		SxD.III
24	Albatros		As.II	121–186	Open		
25–29	FF19		D.I	187	Curtis		
30–39	Ago		100 Gnome	188–200	Open		
40	Albatros		D.I	201–210	FF29	B	D.II
41	FF11		135 Nag	211	FF33	B	D.II
42	Lohner Type M		D.I	212	FF29		D.II
43	Curtis			213–220	FF33	B	D.II
44	Sopwith		200 Salmson	221–230	Albatros	B	Bz.III
45	AEG		Bz.III	231–235	Brandenburg W	BFT	Bz.III
46	Oertz FB3		D.III	236–240	Gotha WD2	B	D.III
47	Rumpler 4E		120 AD	241–253	Rumpler 4B12	B	Bz.III
48	Aviatik WP18		200 hp Argus	254–258	Gotha WD2		D.III
49	Rumpler 4B11		D.I	259	Gotha WD3	BMG	2xD.III
50	Rumpler 4B13		160 Gnome	260–273	Brandenburg W	B	Bz.III
51	Rumpler 4B12		Bz.III	274–275	FF31	CB	Mb.III
52	Albatros		Bz.III	276–280	Oertz W5	CB	Mb.IV
53	Albatros WDD	B	D.III	281	Oertz W6		2xMb.IV
54	Albatros WDD		200 Argus	282–284	Trav. F1	B	D.III
55	Albatros WDD	B	D.III	285–289	Gotha WD1	B	D.I
56	Albatros WDD		Bz.III	290	FF29	B	As.II
57	Brandenburg	B	Bz.III	291–296	FF33D	B	As.II
58	Brandenburg	B/S	D.III	297–299	Open		
59	Gotha WD1		D.I	300	FF35	G	2xD.III
60	Gotha WD2		Bz.III	301–400	Open		
61	Gotha WD2		Rp.III	401	KW Whlm. W1	B	D.I
62	FF27		135 Nag	402	KW Whlm. W2	B	D.I
63	Oertz W4		D.III	403	KW Whlm. W3	B	D.I
64	Rumpler		D.I	404	KW Danzig		D.I
65–69	Ago		As.III	405	KW Danzig	S	D.I

Mr. #	Type	Class	Engine	Mr. #	Type	Class	Engine
406–410	FF29	B	D.II	586	Ago C.IIw	C	Bz.IV
411–415	FF29A	B	D.I	587	FF39	CHFT	Bz.IV
416–421	FF33A	B	D.II	588–590	Brand.KW	CFT/S	Bz.IV
422–423	Brandenburg W	B	Bz.III	591–595	FF33E	BFT	Bz.III
424–425	Gotha WD2	C	D.III	596–600	FF33H	C	Bz.III
426	FF33	B	D.II	601–608	Brand.NW	B	D.III
427–430	Open			609–618	Sablatnig SF2	B	D.III
431	Albatros	B	Bz.III	619	Sablatnig SF3	CHFT	Bz.IV
432	Albatros	B	D.I	620–624	Brand. GW	TMG	2xD.III
433–435	Albatros		Cancelled	625–632	Brand. GNW	B	D.III
436–442	Rumpler 4B12	B	Bz.III	633–637	FF33E	BFT	Bz.III
443–445	LVG	B	D.III	638–642	FF33H	C	Bz.III
446–447	Albatros	B	Bz.III	643–645	FF39	CHFT	Bz.IV
448–449	Open			646–650	Brand. GW	TMG	2xD.III
450	Albatros W2	C	D.III	651–658	Brand. GNW	BFT	D.III
451–455	FF33	B	D.II	659–663	FF33E	BFT	Bz.III
456–458	FF33B	BFT	Mb.III	664–668	FF33H	C	Bz.III
459–460	FF33D	CB	Mb.III	669	FF40	CFT	Mb.IV
461	KW Whlm. W	B	Bz.III	670–676	Gotha WD7	G	2xD.I
462	KW Whlm. W6	B	Bz.III	677	Travemünde F2	CFT	D.IV
463–466	KW Kiel	B	Bz.III	678	FF 41A	TMG	2xBz.III
467–470	KW Danzig	B	Bz.III	679	Gotha WD11	TMG	2xD.III
471–473	FF33C	BFT	D.III	680–684	FF33E	BFT	2xBz.III
474	Oertz W7	C	Mb.III	685–689	FF33H	C	Bz.III
475	Oertz W7	C	D.III	690–694	FF33E	BFT	Bz.III
476	Gotha WD8	C	Mb.IV	695–699	FF33H	C	Bz.III
477	Brandenburg LW	CBMG	D.III	700–704	Brand. GW	TMG	2xD.III
478–483	FF33E	BFT	Bz.III	705–714	Sablatnig SF2	BFT	D.III
484	Lohner T	C	Bz.III	715–724	FF33E	BFT	Bz.III
485	Brandenburg LW	B	D.III	725–729	FF33E	HFT	Bz.III
486–489	Brandenburg NW	B	D.III	730–734	FF33H	C	Bz.III
490	Sablatnig SF1	B	D.III	735	FF	T	2xBz.IV
491–496	FF33E	BFT	Bz.III	736–740	FF33E	BFT	Bz.III
497–508	FF33E	B	Bz.III	741–745	FF33H	C	Bz.III
509	LFG Roland W1	B	Bz.III	746	Brand. GDW	T/G	2xBz.IV
510	FF33H	C	Bz.III	747	Albatros W4	ED	D.III
511–516	Brandenburg FB	C	Bz.III	748	Brand. KDW	ED	Bz.III
517–526	Brandenburg NW	B	D.III	749	FF43	ED	D.III
527	Albatros W3	TMG	2xBz.III	750	LFG W	ED	D.III
528	Brandenburg GW	TMG	2xD.III	751	Rumpler 6B1	ED	D.III
529–533	FF33E	B	Bz.III	752–781	Brand. NW(Go)	B	D.III
534–538	FF33F	B	Bz.III	782	Ursinus-Rex	ED	150 Bz.III
539–540	Ago C.IIw	C	Bz.III	783–784	Brand. KDW	ED	150 Bz.III
541–550	FF33E	BFT	Bz.III	785–786	Albatros W4	ED2MG	150 Bz.III
551	Ru- KW Danzig	B	Bz.III	787–788	Rumpler 6B1	ED	150 Bz.III
552	Brand. Danzig	B	Bz.III	789–790	LFG W	ED	Cancelled
553–562	FF33E	BFT	Bz.III	789–790	FF33S(Rol)	S	D.III
563–570	Brandenburg NW	BFT	D.III	791–800	Sablat. SF2(LVG)	B	D.III
571	Brandenburg LW	C	D.III	801	Gotha WD14	TMG	2xBz.IV
572	Gotha WD9	C	D.III	802–811	FF33E	B	Bz.III
573–577	Gotha WD2	CB	Bz.III	812–821	FF33H	C	Bz.III
578	FBA			822–841	FF33E	HFT	Bz.III
579	Grigorovitch		100 hp Mono.	841	FF33E *Wölfchen* replacement for propoganda		
580–585	Sablatnig SF2	BFT	D.III	842–843	Gotha WD15	B	D.IVa

Mr. #	Type	Class	Engine	Mr. #	Type	Class	Engine
844	Travemünde F3-Refused ED	Bz.III		1289–1298	FF33J	HFT	Bz.III
845–849	Albatros W5	TMG	2xBz.III	1299–1301	LTG FD1	ED	Bz.III
850–859	FF33E	HFT	Bz.III	1302–1326	Albatros W4	ED2MG	D.III
860–869	FF33E	B	Bz.III	1327–1351	Brand. CC	E2MG	Bz.III
870–884	FF33E	HFT	Bz.III	1352–1371	Sablatnig SF5	HFT	Bz.III
885–889	FF33E	B	Bz.III	1372–1379	Gotha WD11	TMG	2xD.III
890–899	Rumpler 6B1	ED	D.III	1380–1394	Brand. KDW	ED	Mb.III
900	Sab. SF4(LVG)	ED	Bz.III	1395–1414	Brand. W12	C2MG	Bz.III
901	Sab. SF4	ED	Bz.III	1415–1430	Gotha WD14	G2MGHFT	2xBz.IVC
902–911	Albatros W4	ED	D.III	1431	Do. Rs.III	R3MG	3xMb.IV
912–921	Brand. KDW	ED	Mb.III	1432	Staaken L	R4MG	3xD.IVa
922–931	FF33J	HFT	Bz.III	1433	Do. Rs.II	R	4xMb.IVa
932	FF33K	C2MG	Bz.III	1434–1458	Rumpler 6B2	ED2MG	D.III
933–941	FF33L	HFT	Bz.III	1459–1468	Sablat. SF5(LFG)	B	Bz.III
942	Roland	BFT	D.III	1469–1471	Brand. W19	C2MG	Mb.IVa
943	Roland W16	CFT	Bz.IV	1472–1474	FF48	C2MG	Mb.IVa
944	Gotha WD12A	BFT	D.III	1475–1477	Sablatnig SF7	C2MG	Mb.IVa
945	KW Whlm. W9	C2MG	Bz.III	1478–1480	Brand. W	Bu	Cancelled
946	Brand. CC	E	Bz.III	1481–1483	Junkers	Bu	Cancelled
947	KW Whlm.	CHFT	D.IV	1484–1513	Albatros W4	ED2MG	D.III
948–967	Albatros W4	E2MG	D.III	1514	Sablatnig SF5	BFT	Bz.III
968–975	Sablatnig SF5	B	Bz.III	1515–1517	Gotha WD20	G2MG	2xD.IVa
976–987	Sablatnig SF5	HFT	Bz.III	1518–1520	LTG FD1	ED	Bz.III
976 (Ersatz)	Repl. original 976	HFT	Bz.III	1521–1535	FF49C	CHFT	Bz.IV
988–990	Brand. W11	ED	Bz.IV	1536–1550	FF49B	BFT	Bz.IV
991–995	Gotha WD11	TMG	2xD.III	1551–1553	Brand. W20	Bu	U.0
996–1000	FF41A	TMG	2xBz.III	1554–1573	Brand. KDW	ED2MG	Mb.III
1001–1010	FF33L	CHFT	Bz.III	1574–1576	Junkers	BFT	Cancelled
1011–1016	Brand. W12	C2MG	D.III	1577–1596	FF33L	C2MG	Bz.III
1017–1036	Sablat. SF5(LVG)	B	Bz.III	1597–1606	FF49C	CHFT	Bz.IV
1037–1061	Rumpler 6B1	ED2MG	D.III	1607–1616	FF49B	BFT	Bz.IV
1062–1066	Rumpler 6B2	ED2MG	D.III	1617–1628	Gotha WD14	G2MGHFT	2xBz.IV
1067–1076	Brand. KDW	ED	Bz.III	1629–1631	Gotha WD	GK2MG	Cancelled
1077–1079	Brand. W16	ED2MG	U.III	1632–1634	Sächsische FW	C2MG	Cancelled
1080–1084	Brand. GW	T/G	2xD.III	1635–1646	Gotha WD	GMGFT	Cancelled
1085–1094	FF33L	CHFT	Bz.III	1647–1649	Brand. W23	EK	D.III
1095–1104	FF33J	HFT	Bz.III	1650	KW Danzig	CHFT	D.IV Cnx
1105	KW Danzig	B/S	Bz.III	1651–1662	Gotha WD14	T/G2MG	2xBz.IV
1106	KW Danzig	C2MG/S	Bz.III	1663–1665	FF53	G2MG	2xD.IVa
1107–1116	Albatros W4	ED2MG	D.III	1666–1668	Open		
1117–1126	FF33L	C2MG	Bz.III	1669–1718	FF49C	CHFT	Bz.IV
1127–1136	FF39	CHFT	Bz.IV	1719–1738	Albatros W4	ED2MG	D.III
1137–1146	Brand. CC	E2MG	Bz.III	1739–1741	Brand. W26	C2MGHFT	D.IVa
1147–1156	Travemünde F2	CHFT	D.IV	1742–1811	FF49C	CHFT	Bz.IV
1157	Oertz W8	CHFT	Mb.IV	1812–1821	FF49C	C2MGHFT	Bz.IV
1158–1177	FF33L	CHFT	Bz.III	1822–1823	FF59C	C2MGHFT	Bz.IV
1178–1187	Brand. W12	C2MG	Bz.III	1824–1841	FF49C	C2MGHFT	Bz.IV
1188–1207	Rumpler 6B2	ED2MG	D.III	1842–1856	FF49C (LFG)	CHFT	Bz.IV
1208–1210	FF41A	T	2xBz.III	1857–1871	Open		
1211–1213	Gotha WD11	TMG	2xD.III	1872–1901	FF49C(Sab)	CHFT	Bz.IV
1214–1223	Sablat. SF5(LVG)	B	Bz.III	1902–1942	Open		
1224–1233	Sablatnig SF5	HFT	Bz.III	1943	Gotha WD	G2MGHFT	Cancelled
1234–1278	FF33L	CHFT	Bz.III	1944–1945	Open		
1279–1288	FF33L	C2MG	Bz.III	1946–1970	Gotha WD14	G2MG	2xBz.IV

Mr. #	Type	Class	Engine
1971–1973	Travemünde F4	CHFT	Bz.IVa
1974–1979	Travemünde F2	CHFT	D.IV
1980–1999	FF33E	S	Bz.III
2000–2019	Brand. W12	C2MG	Bz.III
2020–2022	Sablatnig SF8	S	Bz.III
2023–2052	Brand. W12	C3MG	Bz.III
2053–2092	FF49C	CHFT	Bz.IVa
2093–2112	Brand. W12	C2MG	D.III
2113–2132	Brand. W12	C3MG	D.III
2133–2134	Gotha WD22	G3MG	4xD.III/D.I
2135	Travemünde F4	CHFT	Bz.IVa
2136–2137	Open		
2138	Brand. W.18	E2MG	Bz.III
2139	AEG	R	4xMb.IVa
2140–2200	Open		

Note: To simplify identification of naval aircraft, the following number groups were assigned 16 Nov. 1917:

2201–3000: Hansa-Brandenburg
3001–4000: Friedrichshafen
4001–5000: Gotha
5001–6000: Albatros
6001–6500: Sablatnig
6501–7000: LFG-Bitterfeld
7001–7500: Lübeck-Travemünde
7501–8000: Junkers-Fokker
8001–8500: Staaken
8501–9000: Zeppelin-Lindau
9001–9500: AEG

Hansa-Brandenburg Navy Aircraft Numbers 2201–3000

Marine #	Type	Class	Engine
2201–2203	W27	C3MG	Bz.IIIb
2204	W29	C3MG	Bz.III
2205	W29	C2MG	BMW.IIIa
2206	W29	C3MG	D.III
2207–2216	W19	C3MG	Mb.IVa
2217–2236	W12	C2MGHFT	D.IIIa
2237	W19	CK	Mb.IVa
2238–2257	W19	C3MG	Mb.IVa
2258	W25	ED2MG	Bz.III
2259–2278	W19	C3MG	Mb.IVa
2279–2281	Open		
2282–2284	W32	C3MG	D.IIIa
2285–2286	Brand.W-Cnx	C3MG	D.IVa
2287–2300	W29	C2MGHFT	Bz.III
2301–2302	Brand.W-Cnx	C2MGHFT	3xD.IIIa
2303	Brand.W-Cnx	R	D.I
2304	Brand.W-Cnx	R	D.II
2305	Brand.W-Cnx	G	3xD.IIIa
2306–2307	Brand.W35	G	2xMb.IVa
2308–2500	Open		
2501–2506	W29	C2MGHFT	Bz.III
2507–2536	W29	C3MG	Bz.III
2537	W19	C3MG	Mb.IVa
2538–2540	W33	C3MG	D.IVa
2541	W33	C2MGHFT	Mb.IVa
2542	W33	C3MG	BuS.IVa
2543	W33	CK	BuS.IVa
2544–2563	W19	CK	Mb.IVa
2564–2583	W29	C2MGHFT	Bz.III
2584–2587	W29	C3MG	Bz.IIIa
2588–2589	W29	C2MGHFT	Bz.IIIa
2590–2592	W-Cnx	Bu	Ur.II
2593–2642	W29	C3MG	Bz.III
2543–2652	W29	C3MG	BMW.IIIa
2653–2682	W29	C3MG	Bz.IIIa
2683–2722	W19	C3MG	Mb.IVa
2723–2725	W37	CHFT	Bz.IVa
2726	W33	C3MG	Mb.IVa
2727–2729	W34	C3MG	BuS.IVa
2730–2759	W29	C3MG	Bz.IIIa
2760–2789	W29	C3MG	D.IIIa
2790–2791	W-Cnx	Bu	Ur.II
2792–2800	W	C3MG	D.IVa
2801–3000	Open		
12001–12011	W	C3MG	D.IVa
12012–12041	W-Cnx	C3MG	Mb.IVa
12042–12051	W-Cnx	CK	Mb.IVa
12052–12054	W-Cnx	C3HFT	D.IVa

Friedrichshafen Navy Aircraft Numbers 3001–4000

Marine #	Type	Class	Engine
3001–3030	FF33S	S	Bz.III
3031–3060	FF33J	HFT	Bz.III
3061–3063	FF64	CHFT	D.III
3064–3083	FF49C	CHFT	Bz.IVa
3084–3143	FF49C	CHFT	Bz.IVa
3144–3193	FF33L	C2MG	D.III
3194–3195	FF67-Cnx	B/CHFT	D.IVa
3196	FF-Cnx	CB	D.IVa
3197–3199	FF63-Cnx	CHFT	Bz.IVa
3200	FF-Cnx	CB	D.IVa
3201–3230	FF-Cnx	CHFT	Bz.IVa
3231–3233	FF-Cnx	B/CHFT	D.IVa
3234–3300	Open		
3301–3303	FF60	G	4xD.III
3304–4000	Open		

Gotha Navy Aircraft Numbers 4001–5000

Marine #	Type	Class	Engine
4001–4002	WD28	CHFT	Bz.IVa
4003	WD28	CB	Bz.IVa
4004–4033	FF49C(Go)	C	Bz.IV
4034	WD28	CB	D.IVa
4035–4300	Open		
4301–4325	WD-Cnz	G	2xMb.IVa
4326–4328	WD27	G	4xD.III
4329–5000	Open		

Albatros Navy Aircraft Numbers 5001–6000

Marine #	Type	Class	Engine
5001–5003	W8	C3MG	Bz.IIIb
5001 (Ersatz)	W8 Replacement	C3MG	Bz.IIIb
5004–5006	Alb W-Cnx	CHFT	Bz.IVa
5007–6000	Open		

Sablatnig Navy Aircraft Numbers 6001–6500

Marine #	Type	Class	Engine
6001–6030	SF8	S	Bz.III
6031–6050	FF49C(Sab)	CHFT	Bz.IVa
6051–6080	FF49C(Sab)	CHFT	Bz.IVa
6081–6500	Open		

LFG-Bitterfeld Navy Aircraft Numbers 6501–7000

Marine #	Type	Class	Engine
6501–6520	FF33S(Rol)	S	D.III
6521–6540	FF49C(Rol)	CHFT	Bz.IVa
6541–6543	Roland V19	Bu	Ur.II
6544–6545	Roland	Bu	Ur.II
6546–6800	Open		
6801–6802	Roland	G	Mb.V
6803–7000	Open		

Travemünde Navy Aircraft Numbers 7001–7500

Marine #	Type	Class	Engine
7001–7030	F4	CHFT	Bz.IVa
7031–7040	FF49C(Trav)	CHFT	Bz.IVa
7041–7500	Open		

Junkers Navy Aircraft Numbers 7501–8000

Marine #	Type	Class	Engine
7501–7503	Cs.I	C3MG	Bz.IIIa
7504–7800	Open		
7801–7803		G	2xD.IVa
7804–8000	Open		

Staaken Navy Aircraft Numbers 8001–8500

Marine #	Type	Class	Engine
8001–8300	Open		
8301–8306		R	4xD.IVa
8307		R	4xD.VI
8308–8500	Open		

Dornier Navy Aircraft Numbers 8501–9000

Marine #	Type	Class	Engine
8501–8503	Cs.I	C3MG	Bz.IIIb
8504–8508		Bu	Ur.II
8509–8800	Open		
8801–8802	Rs.IV	R	4xMb.IVa
8803–8804	Rs.-Cnx	R	4xMb.VII
8805–8807	Gs.I	G	2xMb.IVa
8808	Cnx	R	4xMbIVa
8809	Cnx	R	4xMbIVa
8810–9000	Open		

AEG Navy Aircraft Numbers 9001–9500

Marine #	Type	Class	Engine
9001–9300	Open		
9301		R	4xMb.IVa
9302–9303		R	4xMb.IVa
9304–9500	Open		
9501–12000	Open		

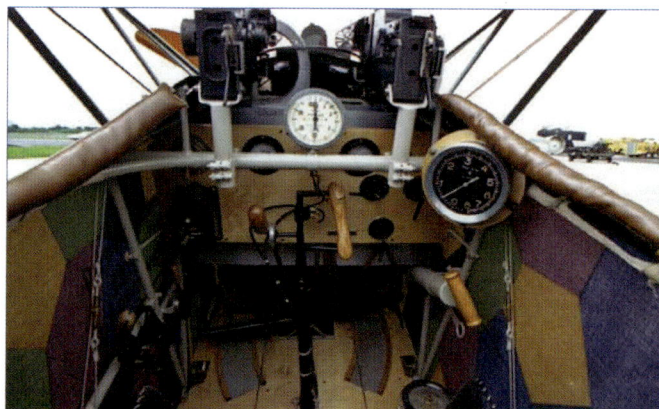

This view of the cockpit of the reproduction Fokker D.VII at the USAF Museum shows the simplicity of these early warplanes. The reverse side of the printed camouflage fabric on the fuselage is clearly visible.

The restored Halberstadt CL.IV at NASM wears the standard factory camouflage and markings for the aircraft built under license by Roland.

Above: This view of the reproduction Fokker D.VII at the USAF Museum shows the standard factory finish of printed camouflage fabric with the striking lilac personal markings of *Lt.* Rudolf Stark, *Jastaführer* of *Jasta* 35b.

Below: The restored Halberstadt CL.IV of the USAF Museum. The colorful markings are those of the commander of *Schlachtstaffel* 21; the other aircraft of *Schlasta* 21 were black with white stripes. The compact cockpit placed the pilot and gunner next to each other, enabling them to communicate and coordinate well during combat.

Kontingentierung
Production Schedule under the *Amerika* Program for January to December, 1918.

Firm	Aircraft Type	Motor Type	Total	Jan.	Feb.	Mar.	Apr.	May	June	July	Aug.	Sep.	Oct.	Nov.	Dec.
Albatros Johan.	Alb. D.Va	D.III or D.IIIa	604	140	170	174	120]	180	154	160	180	180	180	180	180
	Fok. D.VII	D.IIIa	400			6	60								
	D Front Type	D.IIIa	1080							20	20	20	20	20	20
	Alb. J	Bz.IV	355	25	30	30	30	30	30	30	30	30	30	30	30
	Alb. B.IIa or sch.	As.II or D.II	295	65	30	20	20	20	20	20	20	20	20	20	20
Albatros Schneid.	Alb. D.Va	D.III or D.IIIa	500	120	130	148	50	52							
	Fok. D.VII	D.IIIa	200			2	100	98							
	D Front Type	D.IIIa	1050						150	150	150	150	150	150	150
Alb. Warsch.	Alb. D.II?	D.I or D.II	75	25	25	25	]								
AEG	AEG G.IV	D.IVa	120–140	20	25/30	25/30	25/30	25/30							
	G Front Type	D.IVa	175–210						25/30	25/30	25/30	25/30	25/30	25/30	25/30
	AEG J	Bz.IV	400	40	30	30	40	40	40	30	30	30	30	30	30
	AEG N.I	Bz.III	90	50	20	20									
Aviatik Leipzig	Av. C.III	D.III	200		100	100									
	DFW C.V	Bz.IV	300			70	80	80	70						
	C Front Type	Bz.IV or IIIa	360							60	60	60	60	60	60
	Go. GL.VII	D.IVa	100						20	20	20	20	10	10	
	GL Front Type	D.IVa	50							10	10	10	10	10	
	Alb. B.IIa	D.II	90				10	10	10	10	10	10	10	10	10
Ago Johan.	LVG C.II or sch.	D.III	185	30	30	25	20	20	20	20	20]				
	C sch. or Front Type. 70										10	20	20	20	
BFW	Alb. C.Ia	As.III	220	100	100	20									
	Halb. CL.II	D.III	100			60	40								
	C Front Type		480							80	80	80	80	80	80
	Halb. CL.IIa	As.III	200				60	80	60						
Bayru	Ru. C.IV (Bayru)	Bz.IV	275	25	25	25	25	25	25	25	25	25	25	25	
DFW	DFW C.V	Bz.IV	180	50	50	40	40								
	C Front Type	Bz.IV ?	520					50	50	35	35	60	90	100	100
	DFW C.Vc	C.III Nag	350	50	60	40	20	20	40	50	50	20]			
	Alb. C.III	D.III	200		10	10	20	40	20	30	30	30	10]		
Daimler	Fdh G.III	D.IVa	60–85	10	10/15	10/15	10/15	10/15	10/15						
	G Front Type	D.IVa	60–90							10/15	10/15	10/15	10/15	10/15	10/15

Production Schedule under the *Amerika* Program for January to December, 1918.

Firm	Aircraft Type	Motor Type	Total	Jan.	Feb.	Mar.	Apr.	May	June	July	Aug.	Sep.	Oct.	Nov.	Dec.
Euler	LVG B.III	D.I	100	10	15	15	15	15	15	15]					
Friedrichshafen	Fdh G.III	D.IVa	166–186	26	27	23/28	30/35	30/35	30/35						
	G Front Type	D.IVa	180–210							30/35	30/35	30/35	30/35	30/35	30/35
Fokker	Fok. Dr.I	110 Le Rhône	320	60	70	60/70	25/30]								
	Fok. D.VI	110 Le Rhône	120				60	60							
	Fok. D.VII	D.IIIa	230–320			20/30	60/70	60/70	60/70	30/80					
	D Front Type		620–640						60/70	60/70	100	100	100	100	100
	AEG C.IVa	As.III	70	40	30										
Germania	Ru. C.I	Bz.III	95	30	25	20	20								
	Ru. C.Ic	C.III Nag	100					20	20	20	20	20]			
Gotha	Go. G.V	D.IVa	90	15	15	15	15	15	15						
	Go. GL.VII	Mb.IVa	40–75					5	5/10	5/10	5/10	5/10	5/10	5/10	5/10
	G Front Type	D.IVa	90							15	15	15	15	15	15
Hannover	Han. CL.II	As.III	250	80	70	35	45	20]							
	Han. CL.III	D.III	160			65	55	40							
	Han. CL.IIIa	As.III	240					40	90	90	20				
	C Front Type	As.III	430								70	90	90	90	90
Halberstadt	Halb. CL.II	D.III or D.IIIa	470	80	90	100	100	100							
	C Front Type	D.III or D.IIIa	620–660						100	100	100	80/90	80/90	80/90	80/90
Hanseatische	Alb. C.III	D.III	165	25	25	25	25	25	20	20					
Caspar	Fdh G.III	D.IVa	75–140					5	10/15	10/15	10/15	10/15	10/15	10/15	10/15
Junkers	Junk. J.I	Bz.IV	312	15	12	20	25	30	30	30	30	30	30	30	30
	Junk. CL.I	Bz.IV	20				5	10	5						
Kondor	Alb. B.IIa	D.I or D.II	195	25	25	20	20	20	20	20	20	20	5		
LVG Johan.	LVG C.V	Bz.IV	585	135	150	150	150]								
	LVG C.VI	Bz.IV	300					150	150						
	C Front Type	Bz.IV	900							150	150	150	150	150	150
	Go. GL.VII	D.IVa	140					10	20	20	20	20	10?	20?	20?
	Go. G.IV	D.IVa	80	20	20	20	20]								
	LVG B.III	D.II	300	30	30	30	30	30	30	30	30	30	30		
LVG Köslin	Alb. C.III	D.III or Bz.III	240	40	40	40	40	40	40]						

Production Schedule under the *Amerika* Program for January to December, 1918.

Firm	Aircraft Type	Motor Type	Total	Jan.	Feb.	Mar.	Apr.	May	June	July	Aug.	Sep.	Oct.	Nov.	Dec.
LFG	Alb. B.IIa	D.II	450	100	100	100	100	50							
	Han. CL.II	As.III	200						80	100	20				
	Rol. D.VIa or D.VIb	D.IIIa or Bz.IIIa	100				30	30	20	30]					
	C Front Type		480								80	100	100	100	100
Linke	Alb. B.IIa	D.I or D.II	150			30	30	30	30	30]					
Märkische	Ru. C.I	Bz.III	320	50	80	80	80	80	20]						
Merkur	Alb. B.II	D.I	105	35	50	20]									
	Alb. C.Ib	D.III	250			30	50	50	50	50	20]				
Pfalz	Pfal. D.IIIa	D.IIIa	580	140	140	150	150								
	D Front Type	D.IIIa	1200					150	150	150	150	150	150	150	150
	Pfal. D.VII	Sh.III	120			30	90								
	Pfal. D.VIII	Sh.III	125	25	25	25	25	25							
	Pfal. C.I	D.IVa	175						25	25	25	25	25	25	25
	C Front Type														
	D Front Type	Rotation?	480					60	60	60	60	60	60	60	60
Rinne	Ru. C.I	Bz.II	237	25	25	25	25	25	25	25	25	25	12		
Rumpler	Ru. C.IV	D.IVa	180	30	30	30	30	30	30]						
	Ru. C.VII or Rubild Mb	Mb.IVa	280	40	60	60	60	30	30]						
	C or D Front Type		820					40	60	120	120	120	120	120	120
	Ru. D.I	D.III or D.IIIa	50			10	40								
	Ru. C.VIII	As.III	150	50	30	30	20	20							
SSW Berlin	SSW D.III	Sh.III	45–55		1	19	15/20	10/15							
	LVG B.III	D.II	100	10	10	10	15	15	15	15	15	15			
	Go. G.IV	D.IVa	48	10	10	10	10	8]							
	G Front Type		140						20	20	20	20	20	20	20
Shhül	LVG B.IIa	D.I or D.II	180	30	40	30	30	30	20						
	LVG B.III	D.I or D.II	190						10	30	30	30	30	30	30
SSW Nürnb.	Alb. C.III	D.III	110	8	15	15	15	10	10	10	10	10	7]		
Sablatnig	Sab. N.I	As.III	50		10	15	15	10]							
Zeppelin	Zep. CL.I	D.III or D.IIIa	300				15	60	75	75	75				
	C Front Type	D.III or D.IIIa	300									75	75	75	75

German Aircraft Manufacturers & Official Army Abbreviation Where Known

Manufacturer, Location	Official Army Abbreviation
Allgemeine Electrizitäts G.m.b.H., Hennigsdorf bei Berlin	Aeg.
Ago Flugzeug-Werke G.m.b.H., Johannisthal bei Berlin	Ago.
Albatros Werke G.m.b.H., Johannisthal bei Berlin and Friedrichshagen bei Berlin	Alb.
Alter, Ludwig, Werke, Darmstadt	
Automobil und Aviatik A.G., Leipzig-Heiterblick	Av.
Bayerische Flugzeug-Werke A.G., München	Bay.
Bayerische Rumpler-Werke G.m.b.H., Augsburg	Bayru.
Daimler Motorengesellschaft Werke, Sindelfingen	Daim.
Deutsche Flugzeug-Werke G.m.b.H., Lindenthal bei Leipzig	Dfw.
Euler-Werke, Frankfurt am Main, Neiderrad	Eul.
Fokker Flugzeug-Werke G.m.b.H., Schwerin-Gorries in Mecklenburg	Fok.
Flugzeugbau Friedrichshafen G.m.b.H., Manzell and Warnemünde (Zeppelin Subsidiary)	Fdh. *
Goedecker Flugzeug-Werke, Mainz Gonsenheim	
Germania Flugzeug-Werke G.m.b.H., Leipzig-Mockau	Germ.
Gothaer Waggonfabrik A.G., Gotha	Go.
Halberstädter Flugzeug-Werke G.m.b.H., Halberstadt	Halb.
"Hawa" Hannoversche Waggonfabrik A.G., Hannover-Linden	Han.
Hansa und Brandenburgische Flugzeug-Werke G.m.b.H., Priest bei Brandenburg am Havel	
Hanseatische Flugzeug-Werke (Karl Caspar A.G.), Hamburg, Fühlsbüttel	Hansa.
Jeannin Flugzeugbau G.m.b.H., Johannisthal bei Berlin (later became N.F.W.)	
Junkers Flugzeug-Werke A.G., Dessau	Junk.
Junkers-Fokker-Werke (Oct. 1917)	Jfa. or Junk.
Kaiserlich Marineweft (Imperial Dockyards) Reichwerft, Danzig, Kiel and Wilhelmshafen	KW.
Kondor Flugzeug-Werke G.m.b.H., Essen	Kon.
Linke-Hofmann Werke A.G., Breslau.	Li.
Luftfahrzeug Gesellschaft m.b.H., (L.F.G.) Berlin-Charlottenburg.	Rol.
Luft Torpedo Gesellschaft m.b.H., Johannisthal bei Berlin	Torp.
Luft-Verkehrs Gesellschaft m.b.H., Johannisthal bei Berlin	Lvg.
Flugzeugwerft Lübeck-Travemünde G.m.b.H., Travemünde-Privall	
Markische Flugzeug-Werke G.m.b.H., Golm-in-der-Mark	Mark.
Mercur Flugzeugbau G.m.b.H., Berlin	Mer.
Naglo Boots-Werft, Pichelsdorf-Spandau, Berlin	
National Flugzeug-Werke, G.m.b.H., Johannisthal bei Berlin	Nfw.
Nordeutsche Flugzeug-Werke, Tetlow bei Berlin	
Oertz-Werke G.m.b.H., Reiherstieg bei Hamburg	
Ostdeutsche Albatros Werke G.m.b.H., Schneidemuhl.	
(earlier abbreviations sometimes applied Albs. A.W.S.)	Oaw.
Otto-Werke G.m.b.H., Munchen (Munich). (Flugzeug-Werke Gustav Otto.) (Absorbed Bay 1916.)	Ot.
Pfalz Flugzeug-Werke G.m.b.H., Speyer am Rhein	Pfal.
Flugmaschine Rex G.m.b.H., Cologne	
Waggonfabrik Joseph Rathgeber, München-Moosach	Rat.
Albert Rinne Flugzeug-Werke, Rummelsburg bei Berlin	Rin.
Rumpler Flugzeug-Werke G.m.b.H., Johannisthal bei Berlin	Ru.
Sablatnig Flugzeugbau G.m.b.H., Berlin	Sab.
Flugmaschine Fabrik Franz Schneider, Seegefeld bei Spandau	
Luftfahrzeugbau Schutte-Lanz, Mannheim-Rheinau also Zeesen bei Konigswursterhausen	Schül.
Schwade Elugzeug und Motorenbau, Erfurt	
Siemens-Schuckert Werke G.m.b.H., Berlin und Niirnberg	Ssw.
Union Flugzeug-Werke, Teltow bei Berlin	
Zeppelin Aircraft Companies:	
Zeppelin Werke, Lindau G.m.b.H., Reutin and Seemoos (manufacture of Giant "RS" seaplanes)	Do.
Zeppelin Werke Staaken G.m.b.H., Staaken bei Berlin (manufacture of Giant "R" land planes)	Staak.
Flugzeugbau Friedrichshafen G.m.b.H., Manzell and Warnemünde (manufacture of seaplanes)	Fdh.

*Navy designation FF

German and Austrian Aircraft Engines 1914–1918
Table A: German Water-Cooled Inline Engines

No.	Company	Type	Rated HP	RPM	# Cyl.	Form	Bore mm	Stroke mm	Displ. Liters
1	Adler	Ad IV #1	200	2100	8	Dual inline	116	160	13.53
2	Adler	Ad IV #2	200	2100	8	Dual inline	116	160	13.53
3	Argus	As.II	120	1400	6	Inline	130	140	11.15
4	Argus	As.II	120	1400	6	Inline	130	140	11.15
5	Argus	As.III	180	1400	6	Inline	145	160	15.82
6	Argus	As.III impr	180	1400	6	Inline	145	160	15.82
7	Argus	As.IIIa	220	1475	6	Inline	148	165	17.03
8	Argus	As.IV	225	1800	8	V 90°	155	180	27.17
9	Basse & Selve	Bus.II	130/145	1400	6	Inline	125	160	11.78
10	Basse & Selve	Bus.IV	260/270	1400	6	Inline	155	200	22.64
11	Basse & Selve	Bus.IV impr.	270/300	1400	6	Inline	155	200	22.64
12	Basse & Selve	Bus.IVa	275/300	1400/1450	6	Inline	160	200	24.13
13	Basse & Selve	Bus.Vü	300/350	1400	6	Inline	165	200	25.66
14	BMW (Rapp)	Rp.II	145	1400	8	V 90°	140	160	19.70
15	BMW (Rapp)	Rp.III	150	1400	6	Inline	140	160	14.78
16	BMW (Rapp)	Rp.IV	260/300	1400	12	V 60°	140	160	29.56
17	BMW	BMW.II	120	1350	6	Inline	120	160	10.86
18	BMW	BMW.IIIa	185	1410	6	Inline	150	180	19.09
19	BMW	BMW.IV	220	1400	6	Inline	160	190	22.92
20	BMW	BMW.V	400/500	1400	12	V 60°	150	180	38.17
21	BMW	Experim.	400	1300	6	Inline	180	180	27.48
22	BMW Aus.-Daimler	Dm 200 BMW	200	1500	6	Inline	135	175	15.03
23	BMW Aus.-Daimler	Dm 300 BMW	300	1300	12	V 60°	135	175	30.06
24	Benz & Cie.	Bz.II	110	1400	6	Inline	116	160	10.15
25	Benz & Cie.	Bz.III	150	1400	6	Inline	130	180	14.34
26	Benz & Cie.	Bz.IIIa	185	1400	6	Inline	130	190	15.13
27	Benz & Cie.	Bz.IIIav	195	1400	6	Inline	140	190	17.55
28	Benz & Cie.	Bz.IIIaü	225	1400	6	Inline	140	190	17.55
29	Benz & Cie.	Bz.IIIbo	195	1700	8	V 90°	124	140	13.53
30	Benz & Cie.	Bz.IIIbm	200	1800	8	V 90°	135	135	15.46
31	Benz & Cie.	Bz.IIIbv	200	1800	8	V 90°	135	135	15.46
32	Benz & Cie.	Bz.IIIbü	200	1800	8	V 90°	135?	135?	15.46?
33	Benz & Cie.	Bz.IV v1	200	1400	6	Inline	145	190	18.82
34	Benz & Cie.	Bz.IV v2	200	1400	6	Inline	145	190	18.82
35	Benz & Cie.	Bz.IV v3	200	1400	6	Inline	145	190	18.82
36	Benz & Cie.	Bz.IVa v4	225	1400	6	Inline	145	190	18.82
37	Benz & Cie.	Bz.IVau	240	1400	6	Inline	145	190	18.82
38	Benz & Cie.	Bz.V exp	250	1400	12	V 60°	130	180	28.67
39	Benz & Cie.	Bz.V	300	1800	12	V 60°	135	150	25.77
40	Benz & Cie.	Bz.Vb	350	1500	12	V 60°	145	170	33.69
41	Benz & Cie.	Bz.VI	500	1400	12	V 60°	145	200	39.63
42	Benz & Cie.	Bz.VIv	500	1500	12	V 60°	155	200	45.29
43	Benz & Cie.	Bz.VII	600	1400	6	Inline	225	300	71.57
44	Daimler-Mercedes	D.I	100	1400	6	Inline	120	140	9.50
45	Daimler-Mercedes	D.II	120	1400	6	Inline	125	150	11.04
46	Daimler-Mercedes	D.IIa	120	1400	6	Inline	125	150	11.04
47	Daimler-Mercedes	D.III	160	1400	6	Inline	140	160	14.78
48	Daimler-Mercedes	D.III	160	1400	6	Inline	140	160	14.78
49	Daimler-Mercedes	D.IIIa	180	1400	6	Inline	140	160	14.78
50	Daimler-Mercedes	D.IIIav	170	1400	6	Inline	145	160	15.85

Prop RPM	Dry Wt. kg	# In. Vlvs	# Ex. Vlvs	Max HP	Notes	Year	# Built
1150	375	1	1	—	Geared, mag. in back, Pallas carb. side, exp.	1917	—
1150	—	1	1	225	Geared, mag. in front, Pallas carb. in back	1918	1 exp.
—	230	1	1	132	Cudell carb	1913/4	—
—	—	1	1	—	License As.II St.	1917/8	—
—	290	1	1	196	@ 1950 RPM	1915	—
—	—	1	1	—	Zenith alt. carb.	1916	1
—	325	2	2	220	@ 1475 RPM, new design	1916/7	—
1200	350	2	2	250	Prop gear 2:3	1918	—
—	195	1	1	145	@ 1450 RPM. Dev. Kaiser prize, old lube sys.	1914	1
—	400	2	2	—	—	1917	—
—	400	2	2	—	New lube sys.	1917	>300
—	407	2	2	—	High alt. eng.	1917	—
—	415	2	2	350	High alt. eng.	1918	1 exp.
—	300	1	1	—	Dbl. cyl. construct.	1914	—
—	—	1	1	—	Dbl. cyl. construct.	1914	—
—	470	1	1	—	Dbl. cyl. construct.	1915	—
—	210	1	1	140	@ 1400 RPM, Lic. BMW.II Dz.	1918	—
—	285	1	1	260	High alt. eng., n=1580 RPM	1917/8	647
—	295	1	1	265	High alt. eng.	1918/9	5
—	550	1	1	—	Exp., 2x BMW.IIIa	1918/9	1
—	?	?	?	—	Experimental	1917/8	—
—	310	2	2	—	For Austria	—	—
—	460	1	1	—	For Austria	—	—
—	210	1	1	124	@ 1425 RPM, cast cyl	1914/5	510
—	250	1	1	—	Cast cyl.	1914/5	2,995
—	268	2	2	197	Steel cyl, alum. pistons	1916/7	218
—	283	2	2	197	High alt. engine	1917	—
—	—	2	2	239	High alt. eng. improved	1917/8	—
—	—	1	2	225	No gearing	1917	—
1180	—	1	2	260	Gearing, mag in front	1917/8	—
1180	310	1	2	275	N=2000 RPM	1918	—
1180	—	1	2	—	New gearing, mags in rear	1918/9	—
—	340	2	2	225	Induction pipe angled, parallel cooling tubes	1914/5	—
—	—	2	2	—	Induction pipe vert., horiz. Parallel cool tube	1915	—
—	—	2	2	—	Induction pipe angled, cooling tubes xwise	1916/8	7,326
—	—	2	2	—	As above, steel cyl, alum pistons	1917	—
—	370	2	2	—	Over-compressed, steel cyl, alum pistons	1918	—
—	—	1	1	—	2x Bz.III, geared, exp.	1914	1
1180	430	1	2	400	Mags in rear; n=2000 RPM	1918/9	—
985	480	1	2	450	Mags in front; n=1700 RPM	1918/9	—
—	675	2	2	625	Flange for gearing	1916/7	—
—	695	2	2	575/675	Flange for gearing	1917/8	—
—	—	3	3	623	Experimental, 4 plugs/cyl.	1916/7	1
—	190	1	1	105	—	1913/4	—
—	210	1	1	122	—	1914	—
—	200	1	1	136	N=1450 RPM	1915	—
—	275	1	1	170	N=1450 RPM	1915	11,750
?	—	1	1	?	Special design with gear block for Oertz a/c	1914–6	—
—	—	1	1	—	—	1917	—
—	—	1	1	180	—	1917/8	—

No.	Company	Type	Rated HP	RPM	# Cyl.	Form	Bore mm	Stroke mm	Displ. Liters
51	Daimler-Mercedes	D.IIIavü	200	1400	6	Inline	145	160	15.85
52	Daimler-Mercedes	D.IIIa	160	1400	6	Inline	145	160	15.85
53	Daimler-Mercedes	D.IIIa	160	1400	6	Inline	140	160	14.78
54	Daimler-Mercedes	D.IIIb	185	—	8	V 90°	106	170	12.00
55	Daimler-Mercedes	D.IV	220	1400	8	Inline	140	160	19.70
56	Daimler-Mercedes	D.IV	220	1400	8	Inline	140	160	19.70
57	Daimler-Mercedes	D.IVa	260	1400	6	Inline	160	180	21.71
58	Daimler-Mercedes	D.IVa	260	1400	6	Inline	160	180	21.71
59	Daimler-Mercedes	D.IVa	260	1400	6	Inline	160	180	21.71
60	Daimler-Mercedes	D.IVa	260	1400	6	Inline	160	180	21.71
61	Daimler-Mercedes	D.IVa	260	1400	6	Inline	160	180	21.71
62	Daimler-Mercedes	D.IVb	260/350	1400	6	Inline	165	180	23.10
63	Daimler-Mercedes	D.VI	500	1400	18	W 45°	140	160	44.33
64	Daimler-Mercedes	D.VII	600/650	1150/1200	6	Inline	235	250	65.06
65	Conrad	C.III	185	1400	6	Inline	138	190	17.05
66	Conrad	C.IIIa	210	1400	6	Inline	138	190	17.05
67	Körting	Kg.III	185	2150	8	V 90°	—	—	—
68	Körting	Kg.IV	240	1570	12	V 60°	120	140	19.00
69	Körting	Kg.IV	260	1600	12	V 60°	120	140	19.00
70	Man Werke Augsburg	Mana.III	175	1400	6	Inline	140	170	15.70
71	Man Werke Augsburg	Mana.IIIa	185	1400	6	Inline	140	170	15.70
72	Man Werke Augsburg	Mana.IIIav	220	1450	6	Inline	150	170	18.02
73	Man Werke Augsburg	Mana.V	350	1400	10	V 72°	140	170	26.17
74	Maybach	Mb.III (IR)	160	1400	6	Inline	130	150	11.95
75	Maybach	Mb.IV (HSLu)	240	1400	6	Inline	150	180	19.09
76	Maybach	Mb.IVa	240	1400	6	Inline	165	180	23.10
77	Maybach	Mb.IVa	260	1400	6	Inline	165	180	23.10
78	Maybach	Mb.VI	500/520	1400	12	Dbl. Inline	165	180	46.19
79	NAG	C.IIIb Nag	185	1400	6	Inline	138	190	17.05
80	NAG	C.IIIav Nag	185	1400	6	Inline	138	190	17.05
81	Oberursel	U.IVBe	220	2800	8	V 90°	?	?	?

Table B: German Air-Cooled Rotary Engines

No.	Company	Type	Rated HP	RPM	# Cyl.	Form	Bore mm	Stroke mm	Disp. Liters
1	Oberursel	U.0	80	—	7	1 row	124	140	11.83
2	Oberursel	U.I	100	—	9	1 row	124	150	16.30
3	Oberursel	U.III	160	—	14	2 row	124	140	23.67
4	Oberursel	UR.II	110	—	9	1 row	112	170	15.07
5	Oberursel	UR.IIa	115	—	9	1 row	112	170	15.07
6	Oberursel	UR.III	145	—	11	1 row	112	170	18.42
7	Oberursel	UR.IIIa	145	—	11	1 row	112	170	18.42
8	Siemens & Halske	Sh.0	90	—	9	1 row	100	130	9.19
9	Siemens & Halske	Sh.II	110	—	9	1 row	114	130	11.94
10	Siemens & Halske	Versuch(2xSh.0)	180	—	18	2 row	100	130	18.38
11	Siemens & Halske	Sh.III	160	—	11	1 row	124	140	18.60
12	Siemens & Halske	Sh.IIIa	160	—	11	1 row	124	140	18.60
13	Goebel	Goe.II	110	—	7	1 row	138	150	15.71
14	Goebel	Goe.III	160	—	9	1 row	138	200	26.92
15	Goebel	Goe.IIIa	160	—	9	1 row	138	200	26.92
16	Rhemag	UR.II Rhemag	110	—	9	1 row	112	170	15.07
17	Rhemag	Sh.III Rhemag	160	—	11	1 row	124	140	18.60

Notes: 1. Conrad = Deutscher Motorenbau
       2. Maybach = Motorenbau Friedrichshafen

Prop RPM	Dry Wt. kg	# In. Vlvs	# Ex. Vlvs	Max HP	Notes	Year	# Built
—	—	1	1	207	—	1918	—
—	—	1	1	240	Compressor under crank case; n=1600 RPM	1917/8	1
—	—	1	1	—	Chain driven compressor, in Han CL.II	1918	—
?	285	1	1	—	Gearing	1917	272
910	420	1	1	230	—	1915	424
910	420	1	1	230	Removeable gear housing	1916	—
—	—	2	2	—	—	1916	4,502
—	—	2	2	—	Roots compressor under front of engine	1917/8	1
—	—	2	2	—	Schwade compressor on engine rear	1917/8	1
—	—	2	2	—	AEG compressor on engine rear	1917/8	1
—	—	2	2	—	SSW compressor in front	1918	1
—	—	2	2	—	Construction started Sept 1918	1918	—
—	—	1	1	—	No gearing, experimental	1916	1
—	975	2	2	750	N=1250 RPM, glycerine cooling	1916/7	1
—	—	—	—	—	—	—	—
—	336	—	—	—	—	—	—
1075	—	2	2	195	—	1917/8	—
785	—	1	1	252	4 Pallas carbs	1915/6	—
800	—	1	1	—	—	—	—
—	—	1	1	—	—	1916	189
—	—	1	1	—	—	—	—
—	—	1	1	—	—	—	—
—	600	2	2	600	Exp., no gearing	—	—
—	240	2	2	—	—	1914	75
—	245	2	2	—	Developed for airships, then R-planes	1915	550
—	400	2	2	245	High alt., cast iron pistons	Aug 1916	—
—	390	2	2	300	High alt., aluminum pistons	1917/8	—
?	850	2	2	600	2xMbIVa in parallel, experimental	1918	1
—	—	2	2	—	—	—	—
—	—	2	2	—	New design	1918	—
?	260	2	1	230/240	Experimental, geared	1918	1

Prop RPM	Dry Wt. kg	# In. Vlvs	# Ex. Vlvs	Max HP	Notes	Year	# Built
1200	100	X	Z	—	Gnome	1914	—
1200	150	X	Z	—	Gnome	1915	—
1200	190	X	Z	—	Gnome	1915	—
1200	—	Y	Z	—	Le Rhône	1916/7	—
1200	168	Y	Z	—	Le Rhône; high alt.	1917/8	—
1200	—	Y	Z	—	Le Rhône	1917/8	—
1200	—	Y	Z	160	Le Rhône; high alt.	1917/8	—
900<–>	134	X	Z	93.5	Counter-rotary	1916	—
900<–>	140	X	Z	125.7	Counter-rotary	1916/7	218
900<–>	—	X	Z	—	Counter-rotary	—	1
900<–>	194	Y	Z	200	Counter-rotary	1917/8	547
900<–>	—	Y	Z	240	Counter-rotary; over-compressed; high alt.	1918	—
1150/1200	123	X	Z	—	—	End 1916	50
1150	183	X	Z	—	—	—	229
1150	—	X	Z	178	Over-compressed; high alt.	1918	—
1200	—	Y	Z	—	Le Rhône	—	25
900<–>	—	Y	Z	—	Counter-rotary	1918	289

Notes: 1. For rotary valves, X = one valve in piston, automatic; Y = one push rod, Z = one push-rod operated.
2. All Siemens & Halske engines were counter-rotary; engine RPM = 1800, prop RPM = 900.

Table C: Austrian Water-Cooled Inline Engines

No.	Company	Type	Rated HP	RPM	# Cyl.	Form	Bore mm	Stroke mm	Disp. Liters
1	Austro-Daimler	Dm 160	160	1350	6	Inline	135	175	15.03
2	Austro-Daimler	Dm 185	185	1400	6	Inline	135	175	15.03
3	Austro-Daimler	Dm 200	200	1500	6	Inline	135	175	15.03
4	Austro-Daimler	Dm 225	225	1500	6	Inline	135	175	15.03
5	Austro-Daimler	Dm 300	300	1300	12	V 60°	135	175	15.03
6	Austro-Daimler	Dm 345	345	1400	12	V 60°	135	175	15.03
7	Austro-Daimler	Dm 360	360	1500	12	V 60°	135	175	15.03
8	Austro-Daimler	Dm 400	400	—	12	V 60°	—	—	—
9	Austro-Daimler	Dm 500	500	—	12	V 60°	—	—	—
10	Hiero	H 200 (D)	200	1400	8	V 90°	130	180	19.11
11	Hiero	H 220 (D)	220	1400	8	V 90°	130	180	19.11
12	Hiero	H 145 (E)	145	1400	6	Inline	130	160	12.74
13	Hiero	H 150 (E)	150	1400	6	Inline	130	160	12.74
14	Hiero	H 200 (H)	200	1400	6	Inline	135	180	15.46
15	Hiero	H 215 (H)	215	1400	6	Inline	135	180	15.46
16	Hiero	H 230 (H)	230	1400	6	Inline	140	180	16.63
17	Hiero	H 240 (H)	240	1400	6	Inline	140	180	16.63
18	Hiero	H 300 (K)	270/300	1400	6	Inline	155	200	22.64
19	Hiero	H 320 (K)	320	1400	6	Inline	155	200	22.64
20	Hiero	H 350 (K)	350	1400	6	Inline	155	200	22.64

Austrian Engine Abbreviations

First came the abbreviation of the company name, followed by the horsepower in Arabic numerals:
Dm 160 = Austro-Daimler 160 hp
Dm 185 = Austro-Daimler 185 hp
H 145 = Hiero 145 hp
H 230 = Hiero 230 hp
License-built engines were designated as follows:
Dm 185 Mag = Austro-Daimler 185 hp license-built by MAG
Dm 200 Mag = Austro-Daimler 200 hp license-built by MAG
H 200 Fi = Hiero 200 hp license-built by Austro-Fiat
H 230 Lb = Hiero 230 hp license-built by Loeb, etc.

Above: Early production Rumpler C.IV C.6820/16 shows its clean lines. Powered by a 260 hp Mercedes, the C.IV had exceptional ceiling and speed at high altitude.

Above: Late production Rumpler C.IVs lost that elegant spinner but surprisingly gained speed from reduced drag.

Prop RPM	Dry Wt. kg	# In. Vlvs	# Ex. Vlvs	Max HP	Notes	Year	# Built
—	288	1	1	—	Lic. Mag	1914	—
—	298	1	1	—	Lic. Mag	1914/5	—
—	310	2	2	—	Lic. BMW, Mag	1915/6	—
—	310	2	2	—	Lic. BMW	1916/7	—
—	460	1	1	—	—	1916/7	—
—	465	1	1	—	—	1917/8	—
—	465	1	1	—	—	1918	—
—	—	—	—	—	Lic. Pr.	1918	—
—	—	2	2	—	—	1918	—
—	260	1	1	—	Lic. Bd, Fi	1914	—
—	270	1	1	—	Lic. Mar	—	—
—	215	1	1	—	—	1914	—
—	205	1	1	180	—	1914	—
—	315	1	1	—	Lic. Lb	1915	—
—	315	1	1	—	—	1915	—
—	340	2	2	—	Lic. Gf, Fi, Lb	1916	—
—	340	2	2	270	—	1916/7	—
—	400	2	2	—	—	1918	—
—	400	2	2	—	Incr. Comp.	1918	—
—	400	2	2	—	Incr. Comp.	1918	—

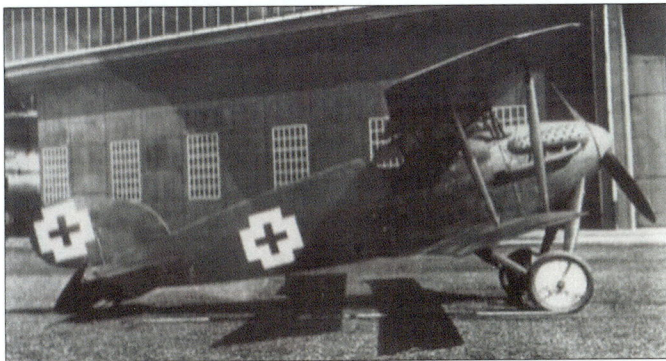

Above: The Daimler D.I fighter prototype was powered by Daimler's Mercedes D.IIIbm V-8 engine. German V-8 engines entered production too late to power any aircraft that reached the front.

Above: The Roland D.XVII prototype fighter powered by the 185 hp BMW.IIIa competed at the Third Fighter Competition. By mid-1918 the monoplane configuration was popular for German fighter designs.

Right: Clearly inspired by the Brandenburg monoplanes, the all-metal Dornier Cs.I takes off on a test flight. Bulky ear radiators are fitted to expedite testing, but a nose radiator was soon fitted for lower drag.

German Aircraft Engine Manufacturers, 1914–1918

All engines water-cooled inline designs except where noted * for air-cooled rotary or ** for both types.

#	Abbrev.	Company	Original Design	License
1	Ad	Adler-Werke, formerly H. Kleyer A. G., Frankfurt a/M	Yes	—
2	As	Argus-Motoren-Gesellschaft m.G.H., Berlin-Reinickendorf	Yes	—
3	BuS	Basse & Selve, Altena (Westfalen)	Yes	D.III BuS
4	BMW	Bayerische Motoren Werke A. G., München	Yes	For Austria; Dm 200 BMW, Dm 300 BMW
5	Bz	Benz & Cie., Rheinische Automobil-und-Motoren-Fabrik, Mannheim	Yes	—
6	D	Daimler-Motoren-G.m.b.H., Stuttgart-Untertürkheim	Yes	—
7	C	Deutsche-Motorenbau-Gesellschaft G.m.b.H., (Conrad), Berlin-Marienfelde	Yes	—
8	Dz	Gasmotoren-Fabrik-Deutz, Köln-Deutz	No	As.III Dz; BMW II Dz (385 built)
9*	Goe	Gnadenbergerische Maschinenfabrik, Inh. Georg Goebel, Darmstadt	Yes	—
10	Gü	Güldener-Motoren-Gesellschaft, Aschaffenburg	No	As.III Gü (124 built)
11	Kg	Gebrüder Körting A.G., Hannover-Körtingsdorf	Yes	—
12	Loeb	Loeb Werke A. G., Automobil-und-Flugmotoren-Fabriken, Berlin, Werk I=Charlottenburg, Werk II=Hohenschönhausen	No	For Austria: H 200 Lb, H 230 Lb
13	Man	Maschinenfabrik Augsburg-Nürnburg A.G. Abteilung Flugmotoren, Werk = Augsburg	Yes	—
14	Man	Maschinenfabrik Augsburg-Nürnburg A.G. Abteilung Flugmotoren, Werk=Nürnburg	No	As.III Man (395 built)
15	Mb	Motorenbau G.m.b.H., Friedrichshafen a/ B (Maybach)	Yes	—
16**	U	Motorenfabrik Oberursel A.G., Oberursel	Yes	—
17	Nag	Nationale Automobil-Gesellschaft, Berlin-Oberschöneweide	No	C.III Nag, D.III Nag
18	NSU	Neckarsulmer Fahrzeugwerke A. G., Neckarsulm	No	Mb.IVa NSU (150 built)
19	O	Adam Opel, Rüsselheim	Yes	As.III O (1,975 built), BMW.IIIa O (287 built)
20	Rp	Rapp-Motoren-Werke G. m. b. H., (became BMW July 20, 1917)	Yes	—
21*	Rhemag	Rhemag-Rhenania Motoren-Fabrik A. G., Mannheim	No	UR.II Rhemag (25 built), Sh.III Rhemag (289 built)
22	Rie	L. A. Riedinger, Augsburg	No	D.IIIa Rie, D.IIIav Rie
23*	Sh	Siemens Halske A. G., Berlin-Siemensstadt	Yes	—
24	St	Stoewer-Werke A. G., Berlin	No	As.II St., As.III St (812 built)
25	Sw	Otto Schwade Co., Erfurt	No	BuS.IVa Sw
26	Un	Union-Werke A. G., Mannheim	No	—

German Engine Abbreviations

Horsepower was signified by Roman Numerals as follows:

0 = Under 100 hp
I = 100 hp
II = over 100 hp to 150 hp
III = over 150 hp to 200 hp
IV = over 200 hp to 300 hp
V = over 300 hp to 400 hp

If a firm produced several different engines in the same horsepower class, than a small letter suffix was placed after the Roman numeral as outlined below:

D.IV = 220 hp 8-cylinder Mercedes
D.IVa = 260 hp 6-cylinder Mercedes
Bz.III = 150 hp 6-cylinder Benz
Bz.IIIa = 180 hp 6-cylinder Benz (improved)
Bz.IIIb = 195 hp 8-cylinder Benz V-8, etc.

License-built types were designated as follows:
180 hp Argus = As III
180 hp Argus license-built by Opel = As III O
180 hp NAG license-built by Conrad = C.III Nag, etc.

Austrian Aircraft Engine Manufacturers

#	Abbrev.	Company	Original Design	License
1	Dm	Österreichische Daimler Motoren A.G., Wiener-Neustadt	Yes	—
2	H	Österreichische Industriewerke Warchalowski, Eissler & Co., Wien	Yes	—
3	Bd	Maschinenbau A. G. form. Breitfeld, Danek Co., Prague	No	Hiero
4	Fi	Österreichische Fiat-Werke A. G., Wien (Vienna)	No	Hiero
5	Gf	Ganz-Fiat Ungarische Flugmotorenfabrik A.G., Budapest	No	Hiero
6	Mag	Ungarische Allgemeine Maschinenfabrik A.G. (MAG), Budapest	No	Austro-Daimler
7	Mar	Ungarische Automobil A.G. (Marta), Arad	No	Hiero, Benz Bz.IV
8	Pr	Erste Böhmisch-Mährische Maschinenfabrik (Praga), Prague	No	Austro-Daimler
9*	St	Österreichische Waffenfabrik A.G., Steyr	No	Oberursel Ur.II

German Manufacturers that Built Austrian Engines Under License

#	Abbrev.	Company	Original Design	License
10	BMW	Bayerische Motoren Werke A. G., München	Yes	Dm 200 BMW, Dm 300 BMW
11	Lb	Loeb & Co. G.m.b.H., Berlin (later Loeb Werke A. G., Berlin)		NoH 200 Lb, H 230 Lb

Other Aircraft Engines Used by the Austrians

#	Abbrev.	Company	Type
12	Bz	Benz Cie., Mannheim	Bz.IV
13	Merc	Daimler-Motoren-Gesellschaft m.b.H., Stuttgart	D.I, D.II
14	Rp	Rapp-Motoren-Werke G. m. b. H., Munchen	Rp V-8 145 hp
15	Ob	Motorenfabrik Oberursel A. G. , Oberursel	—
16	Sh	Siemens Halske A. G. Berlin-Siemensstadt	Sh.II, Sh.III
17	Gn	Société des Moteurs Gnôme, Paris (from pre-war)	—
18	Rh	Société Anonyme des Moteurs Le Rhône, Paris (from pre-war)	—

German Engines Built in Switzerland During the War

#	Abbrev.	Company	Type
19	B	Seebacher Maschinen A.G., Seebach-Zürich (Reinhold Becker) Horgen bei Zürich	As.III B
20	SLM	Schweizerische Lokomotive-u. Maschinenfabrik A.G., Winterthur (built only for Switzerland)	As.II SLM

Right: Replica Fokker Triplane in the markings of Lothar von Richthofen of *Jasta* 11. The red struts, wheel covers, and cowling are the *Jasta* 11 markings; the yellow tail and top wing are Lothar's personal markings.

German Aircraft Inventory as of 21 December, 1917

	Type	Number on Hand	Number to Be Delivered		Type	Number on Hand	Number to Be Delivered
AEG	B.II	2	0		C.X	86	0
	C.I	10	0		C.X(Bayr)	33	0
	C.II	12	0		C.X(Ls)	49	0
	C.IV	339	20		C.X(OAW)	77	0
	C.IV(Fok)	162	18		C.X(Rol)	89	0
	C.IVa(Fok)	15	185		*Total C.X*	*334*	*0*
	DJ.I	0	3		C.XII	145	69
	G.II	9	0		C.XII(Bayr)	146	27
	G.III	16	0		*Total C.XII*	*291*	*96*
	G.IV	55	94		D.II	155	0
	G.IVk	0	5		D.II(LVG)	54	0
	J.I	91	50		*D.II Total*	*209*	*0*
	N.I	90	41		D.III	362	11
					D.III(OAW)	684	61
Ago	C.I	9	0		*Total D.III*	*1046*	*72*
	C.IV	170	3		D.V	602	7
	C.IV(Schül)	45	0		D.Va	7719	751
					G.III	6	0
Albatros	B.I	59	0		J.I	56	67
	B.II	271	5				
	B.II(Bay)	185	29	**Aviatik**	B.I	17	0
	B.II(Kon)	188	0		B.II	8	0
	B.II(Refl)	126	61		C.I	157	4
	B.II(Merk)	371	42		C.I(Han)	53	0
	B.II(Rol)	239	1		*Total C.I*	*210*	*4*
	Total B.II	*1380*	*138*		C.II	43	0
	B.IIa	71	179		C.III	150	69
	B.IIa(Li)	0	150				
	B.IIa(Kon)	13	137	**DFW**	C.I	22	0
	B.IIa(Rol)	316	283		C.V	761	172
	Total B.IIa	*400*	*949*		C.V(Av)	632	164
	B.III	100	0		C.V(Halb)	111	1
	C.I	281	0		C.V(LVG)	236	5
	C.I(Rol)	39	0		*Total C.V*	*1740*	*342*
	C.I(Merk)	0	250		C.Vc	31	269
	Total C.I	*320*	*250*				
	C.Ia	208	90	**Euler**	B.I	9	0
	C.Ib	0	250		C.I	3	0
	C.III	477	11		D.I	18	0
	C.III(DFW)	0	200		D.II	94	1
	C.III(Bayr)	439	4				
	C.III(Ls)	13	1	**Fokker**	D.II	132	0
	C.III(LVG)	137	161		D.III	159	0
	C.III(SSW)	0	100		D.IV	33	0
	C.III(Hansa)	45	152		D.V	216	0
	Total C.III	*1121*	*629*		D.VI	0	120
	C.V	84	0		D.VII	0	300
	C.VI	42	0		D.VII(Alb)	0	400
	C.VII	220	0		*Total D.VII*	*0*	*700*
	C.VII(Bayr)	126	0		Dr.I	173	140
	Total C.VII	*346*	*0*		E.I	19	0

	Type	Number on Hand	Number to Be Delivered		Type	Number on Hand	Number to Be Delivered
	E.II	3	0	**Otto**	C.II	2	0
	E.III	96	0		C.II(LVG)	2	0
					Total C.II	*4*	*0*
Friedrich-shafen	G.II	5	0				
	G.II(Daim)	9	0	**Pfalz**	C.I	36	260
	Total G.II	*14*	*0*		D.III	323	14
	G.III	93	77		D.IIIa	382	457
	G.III(Daim)	38	56		E.I	38	0
	G.III(Hansa)	0	35		E.II	95	0
	Total G.III	*131*	*168*		E.VI	8	0
	N.I	0	3				
				Roland	C.II	28	0
Gotha	G.III	10	0		C.IIa	27	0
	G.IV	12	0		C.IIa(Li)	16	0
	G.IV(LVG)	81	2		*Total C.IIa*	*43*	*0*
	G.IV(SSW)	29	35		C.XI	0	3
	Total G.IV	*122*	*37*		D.I	13	0
	G.V	65	61		D.I(Pfal)	8	0
					Total D.I	*21*	*0*
Halberstadt	B.II	2	0		D.II	20	0
	B.III	3	0		D.II(Pfal)	11	0
	CL.II	364	315		*Total D.II*	*31*	*0*
	CL.II(Bayr)	0	100		D.IIa	163	0
	Total CL.II	*354*	*415*		D.IIa(Pfal)	118	0
	D.III	29	0		*Total D.IIa*	*281*	*0*
	D.V	41	0		D.III	98	3
					D.VIa	0	53
Hannover	CL.II	354	128				
	CL.II(Rol)	0	200	**Rumpler**	B.I	49	0
	Total CL.II	*354*	*328*		C.I	231	0
	CL.III	0	200		C.I(Germ)	118	60
					C.I(Hansa)	60	2
Junkers	J.I	36	114		C.I(Mark)	374	120
					C.I(Rin)	82	214
LVG	B.I	63	0		*Total C.I*	*865*	*405*
	B.I(Ot)	16	0		C.Ia(Han)	325	0
	Total B.I	*79*	*0*		C.Ic	0	100
	B.II	77	0		C.III	27	0
	B.II(Ot)	2	0		C.IV	305	125
	B.II(Schül)	61	139		C.IV(Bayr)	73	274
	Total B.II	*140*	*139*		*Total C.IV*	*378*	*398*
	B.III	0	300		C.V	16	1
	B.III(Eul)	0	100		Rubild	83	7
	B.III(Schül)	0	300		C.VII	92	202
	B.III(SSW)	0	100		C.VIII	94	125
	Total B.III	*0*	*800*		C.IX	17	5
	C.I	33	0		G.II	9	0
	C.II	278	2		G.III	21	46
	C.II(Ago)	9	191				
	Total C.II	*287*	*193*	**SSW**	D.I	45	0
	C.IV	34	0		D.II	0	2
	C.V	97	233				
				Zepp.-W	D	0	3

German Warplane Production by Class

Source: The Development of German Army Aircraft in the War by Dr.-Ing. Wilhelm Hoff, *Zeitschrift des Vereines Deutscher Ingenieure*, 1920, p.493, translated by the Office of Naval Intelligence, Navy Department, Washington, DC, as National Advisory Committee for Aeronautics Technical Note No. 56.

Class	1911	1912	1913	1914	1915	1916	1917	1918	Total
A	11	60	168	294	13	22			568
B	13	76	278	1,054	1,312	440	2993	25	6,191
C					2,674	4,726	10,337	7,320	25,057
D					1	2,129	4,945	5,132	12,207
Dr							338	1	339
E					347	300		381*	1,028
G					185	465	589	789	2,028
J							450	463	913
N						100	94	10	204
S								2	2
Total	24	136	446	1348	4,532	8,182	19,746	14,123	48,537

* Mostly Fokker E.V, which were later re-designated Fokker D.VIII. About 80 R-types were built but not listed.

When researching German aviation production in WW1, it immediately becomes clear that no source is definitive. The loss of the War Archives in Potsdam due to bombing in WW2 means the source material that might have provided definitive information is lost. All other sources give different quantities, and the exact facts remain unknown. Consequently, the source of the numbers on this page is cited for the reader's benefit. In addition to Army aircraft, about 2,365 aircraft were produced for the Navy. These numbers are similar, but not identical, to the German production numbers given on page 4. Note that CL types are not called out in the table above; were they included in the C-types? Similarly, GL types are not shown separately, and R types and Naval aircraft (about 2,365) are not shown.

In contrast, Austrian production numbers are known with greater precision. Estimates of Austrian

German Aero Engine Production

Period	Inline Engines	Rotary Engines	Total
Aug.–Dec.1914	748	100	848
1915	4,544	493	5,037
1916	6,930	892	7,822
1917	10,364	836	11,200
1918 (full year)	13,757	1,785	15,542
Total	**36,343**	**4,106**	**40,449**

aero-engine production vary from 4,518 to 4,902 depending on the source. However, the Austrian Army accepted 4,768 aircraft, and the Navy accepted 413 aircraft. In addition, 125 prototypes were built, and 20 of those were accepted by the Army and are included in that total. These numbers total 5,181 aircraft accepted plus 105 prototypes, or a total of 5,286 Austrian warplanes built during WW1.

Bibliography
Books
Davilla, Dr. James J., *French Aircraft of the First World War*, Stratford: Flying Machines Press, 1997.

Grosz, Peter M., Haddow, George, and Schiemer, Peter, *Austro-Hungarian Army Aircraft of World War One*, Mountain View, 1993.

Gary, Peter, and Thetford, Owen, *German Aircraft of the First World War*, second revised edition, New York: Doubleday & Company, Inc., 1970.

Herris, Jack, *Pfalz Aircraft of World War I*, Boulder: Flying Machines Press, 2001.

Herris, Jack, and Pearson, Bob, *Aircraft of World War I: 1914–1918*, London: Amber Books Ltd., 2010.

Articles
Grosz, Peter M., "Frontbestand" *WW1 Aero* No.107, Dec. 1985, p.60–66.

Grosz, Peter M., "Frontbestand" *WW1 Aero* No.108, Feb. 1986, p.66–69.

Hoff, Dr.-Ing. Wilhelm, "The Development of German Army Aircraft in the War", *Zeitschrift des Vereines Deutscher Ingenieure*, 1920, p.493, translated by the Office of Naval Intelligence, Navy Department, Washington, DC, as National Advisory Committee for Aeronautics Technical Note No. 56.

Reddehase, Erwin, "German and Austrian Aircraft Engines of the First World War", *Cross & Cockade*, Vol.5 No.4, Winter 1964, p.321–326.

Glossary of Terms

Abteilung: Unit, detachment, or section
Amerikaprogramm: America program
Armee Flug Park (AFP): Army aviation supply depot
Armee Korps: Army Corps
Armee Oberkommando (AOK): Army headquarters
Artillerie Flieger Abteilung: Artillery flying unit
Artilleriefliegerschule: Artillery flying school
Artillerie Prüfungs Kommission (APK): Artillery examination board
Asienkorps: Asian Corps

Ballonzug: Balloon platoon
Baltkchen Landeswehr: Baltic militia
Bombenflugzeuggeschwader: Bombing aeroplane squadron
Bombengeschwader: Bombing squadron
Bombenstaffel: Bombing echelon
Brieftauben Abteilung Metz (B.A.M.): Carrier pigeon unit Metz
Brieftauben Abteilung Ostende (B.A.O.): Carrier pigeon unit Ostend

Chef des Feldflugwesens (Feldflugchef): Chief of Field Aviation
Chef des Generalstabes des Feldheeres: Chief of the General Staff of the Armies in the Field

Deutsche Luftamt: German Aviation Authority
Deutsche Luftschiffahrts Aktiengesellschaft (Delag): German Airship Transport Company

Ehrenbecher Dem Sieger im Luftkampf: Cup of Honor for the victor in aerial combat
Eisenbahntruppe: Railway troops
Etappen Flugzeugpark: Aeroplane supply depot in the army communications zone
etatsmässig: worthy of being included in the military budget

Feldartillerie Ersatz Abteilung: Field artillery supply unit
Feldflieger Abteilung: Field aviation unit
Feldluftschiffer Abteilung: Field aviation unit (lighter-than-air)
Feldlufkchffer Abteilung Stäbe: The staff of more than one Field lighter-than-air aviation unit
Feldluftschfferpark: Depot for lighter-than-air field aviation
Feldluftschiffertruppe: Field lighter-than-air-aviation troops
Festungsflieger Abteilung: Fortress or garrison flying unit

Festungsluftschiffer Trupps: Fortress or garrison aviation troop (lighter-than-air)
Flak Ersatz Abteilung: Anti-aircraft artillery supply unit
Flaktruppe: Anti-aircraft troops
Flieger Abteilung: Aviation unit or section
Flieger Abteilung (A): Aviation unit for co-operation with the artillery
Flieger Abteilung (A) (No) Lb: As above but equipped with special camera equipment for photographic reconnaissance
Flieger Abteilung Pascha: Aviation unit formed for use in the Middle East
Flieger Ersatz Abteilung: Aviation replacement unit
Flieger Kommando Döberitz: Aviation detachment at Döberitz
Flieger Depot: Aviation depot
Fliegerkammer: Aerial camera
Flieger Kompanie: Aviation company
Fliegerkorps der Obersten Heeresleitung: Flying corps of the Army High Command
Fliegerschule: Flying school
Fliegerstation: Military aerodrome or air station
Flugabwehrkanonen (Flak): Anti-aircraft artillery
Flugmeldedienst: Organisation for reporting aerial activity
Flugpark Kurland: Aviation depot in Kurland (1919)
Fokker Gestänge Steuerung: Fokker pushrod control
Freiherr: Baron
Freiwilligen Reserve Korps: Volunteer reserve corps

Gardekorps: Corps of Guards
Garde Infanterie Regiment: Guards Infantry Regiment
Gaskolonne: Gas Transport Column
General der Infanterie: General of Infantry
Generafeldmarschall: Field Marshal
Generalinspektion des Militärverkehtswesens: Inspector General's department of military transport
General Inspektion des Militärverkehrstruppen: General Inspectorate of military transport troops
Generalleutnant: Lieutenant General
Generalquartiermeister: Quartermaster General
Geschwaderführer: Squadron leader
Geschwadern: More than one squadron
Gruppenführer der Flieger (Gruf): Officer attached to Corps HQ responsible for the best utilisation of the aviation units assigned to the Corps. (Group leader of aviation)

Hauptmann: Captain

Heeresgruppenkommando F: Army Group detachment F

Heereswetterdienst: Army Meteorological Service

Heimatluftschutz: Homeland aerial defence

Infanterieflieger (If): Infantry co-operation aircraft

Infanterie Regiment 95: Infantry Regiment No. 95

Inspekteur: Inspector

Inspektion der Fliegertruppen (Idflieg): Inspectorate of military aviation

Inspektion der Flugabwehrkanonen im Heimatgebiete (Iftakheim): Inspectorate of anti-aircraft artillery in the home area

Inspektion der Luftschiffertruppen (Ilust): Inspectorate of military aviation (lighter-than-air)

Inspektion der Verkehrstruppen: Inspectorate of transport troops

Inspektion des Militär Luft und Kraftfahrwesens: Inspectorate of Military Aviation and Motor Transport

Jagdgeschwader: Permanent grouping of four *Jagdstaffeln* having a total strength of approximately 50 aeroplanes

Jagdgruppe: Non-permanent grouping of a number of *Jagdstaffeln* giving a total strength of between 36 and 75 single-seat fighters

Jagdstaffel: Fighter section or fighter unit

Kampfeinsitzer Abteilung: Single-seat fighter unit

Kampfeinsitzer Kommando Vaux: Single-seat fighter detachment at Chateau Vaux near St. Quentin

Kampfgeschwader der Obersten Heeresleftung (Kagohl): Fighting Squadron of the Army High Command

Kampfflugzeug: Fighting aeroplane

Kampfstaffeln (Kasta): Fighting sections

Ketten: Groups of two or three aircraft flying together

Kommandeur der Flieger (Kofl): Officer in charge of all the flying units assigned to an Army

Kommandeur der Luftschiffer (Koluft): Officer in charge of all flying units (lighter-than-air) assigned to an Army

Kommandeur der Flugabwehrkanonen (Koftak): Officer in charge of all anti-aircraft artillery assigned to an Army

Kommandeur: Commander

Kommandierenden General der Luftstreitkräfte (Kogenluft): General in command of the German Army Air Service

Kommando, Detachment Konigin Elisabeth Garde Grenadier Regiment Nr 3: Queen Elizabeth Grenadier Guards Regiment No.3

Kraftwagengeschütze: Artillery piece mounted on a motor lorry chassis

Kraftwagenflak (K-Flak): Anti-aircraft gun mounted on a motor lorry chassis

Kriegsakademie: War Academy

Kriegsministerium: War Ministry

Lb Flugzeug: Aeroplane fitted with special camera equipment

Lehr und Versuchsanstaltfür Militärflugwesen: Training and Experimental Establishment for Military Aviation

Leichtmaschinengevvehr (LMG): Light machine gun

Leipziger lllustrierte Zeitung: Leipzig Illustrated Newspaper

Leutnant der Reserve: 2nd Lieutenant of the Reserve

Lehr und Versuchsabteilung für Lichtbildwesen: Training and Experimental Detachment for Photography

Leutnant: 2nd Lieutenant

Lichtbild (Lb): Photograph

Luftfahrzeug im Heeresdienst: Aircraft in Army Service

Luftschiff: Airship

Luftschiffer Abteilung: Lighter-than-air aviation unit

Luftschiffer Abteilung der Versuchsabteilung der Verkehrstruppen: Lighter-than-air-section of the Experimental Detachment of the Transport troops

Luftschiffer Bataillon: Lighter-than-air Battalion

Luftschiffer Detachement: Lighter-than-air Detail

Luftschiffer Ersatz Abteilung: Aviation supply unit (lighter-than-air)

Luftschffertruppe: Aviation troop or Military Aviation (lighter-than-air)

Luftschiff Kommando: Airship Detachment

Luftstreitkräfte: Air Force or Air Service

Luftwaffe: Air Weapon or Air Force

Militarluftschiff: Military Airship

Modell: Model

Nationalflugspende: National Fund for the promotion of aviation

Oberleutnant: Lieutenant

Oberst: Colonel

Obersten Heeresleitung (OHL): Army High Command

Oberstleutnant: Lieutenant Colonel

Offizierstellvreter: Warrant Officer

Ostpreussischen Freiwilligen Korps: East Prussian Volunteer Corps

Pfeil: Arrow

Pistolenkammer: Aerial camera with a pistol grip

Polizei Flieger Staffeln: Police Aviation Sections

Prüfanstalt und Werft (PuW): Test Establishment and Workshop

Reichskanzler: Chancellor
Rekhswehr: German military forces from 1919–1935
Reichswehr Flieger Staffeln: German Military Aviation Sections (1919)
Reihenbildner (Rb): Aeroplane fitted with camera for strip overlap work, or sequence camera
Reihenbildzug: Detachment of usually three special camera aircraft within a *Flieger Abteilung*
Riesenflugzeug Abteilung: Unit equipped with giant aeroplanes of the R Category
Reserve Korps: Reserve Corps
Reserve Korps Kowno: Reserve Corps formed in the Kowno area on the Eastern Front
Ritter: Knight
Rittmeister: Cavalry Captain

Schlachtgeschwader: Battle Squadron (Permanent grouping of 4 or 6 *Schlachtstaffeln*)
Schlachtstaffeln: Battle sections
Schlachtgruppen: Non-permanent grouping of a number of *Schlachtstaffeln*
Schutzstaffel (Schusta): Unit or section of two-seat aeroplanes for the protection of artillery or army co-operation two-seaters
Selbstladegewehr: Semi-automatic rifles of 10-shot capacity
Soldatenrat: Soldiers Council
Spinne: Spider
Stab: Staff
Stabsbildabteilungen (Stabia): Staff Photographic unit for the evaluation of reconnaissance photographs
Stabsoffizier der Flieger (Stofl): Staff Officer for Aviation within an Army
Stabsoffizier der Luftschiffer (Soluft): Staff Officer for aviation (lighter-than-air) within an Army
Staffelführer: Leader of a section or unit
Staffeln: Detachments, Sections or Echelons

Taube: Pigeon

Uebungs Flieger Abteilung: Practice Flying Unit
Unteroffizier: Non-commissioned officer

Verkehrstechnischen Prüfungskommission: Technical Transport Examination Board
Verkehrstruppen: Transport Troops
Versuchsabteilung der Verkehrstruppen: Experimental Section of Transport Troops
Vizefeldwebel: Sergeant Major

Werke: Works
Wetterdienst: Weather Service

The famous Fokker Triplane was too slow to be a general success, but its maneuverability and climb made it a mainstay of German aces until the Fokker D.VII arrived. These are serving with *Jasta* Boelcke.

The unarmed B-types (a Rumpler above) were essential reconnaissance aircraft. The evolution of air combat required them to gradually be replaced by armed two-seaters, the C-types.

The giant Staaken bombers were the largest operational WWI airplanes. Staaken R.V serial 13/15 was powered by five 245 hp Maybach Mb.IVa engines; one was in the nose and two in each nacelle geared to drive a single propeller.

Above: Reproduction of the single most famous WWI airplane, the Fokker Triplane that Manfred von Richthofen, the Red Baron flew on his fatal mission.
Left: Manfred (at right) and Lothar (at left) von Richthofen in March 1918.
Below: Beautiful reproduction Fokker Triplane in authentic camouflage and markings for Lothar von Richthofen. Lothar, a 40-victory ace, was the Red Baron's younger brother. The yellow rear fuselage and top of the upper wing were his personal markings; the red cowling, struts, and wheel covers were the markings for *Jasta* 11.

Made in the USA
Charleston, SC
26 September 2013